I0101153

# MASTERS MASHUPS
## From Shakespeare to Stephen King

# MASTERS MASHUPS
## From Shakespeare to Stephen King

by Melissa G Wilson

Copyright Networlding Publishing, 2015

ISBN 13: 978-0-9883471-4-4

All rights reserved.

net worlding
PUBLISHING

# MELISSA G WILSON

# MASTERS MASHUPS

## FROM SHAKESPEARE TO STEPHEN KING

PART OF THE **MASTERS MASHUPS** SERIES

# TABLE OF CONTENTS

**Chapter 1. Mashups? We Begin** ..................................... 7

Why Should You Care? Because Mashups Create
More to Ponder and Tickle Your Brain!                  8

**Chapter 2. Stephen King And The King Of
Sonnets: The Works** .........................................17

*Titus Andronicus* and *Carrie*                        **21**
*Hamlet* and *The Shining*                             **28**
*Richard III* and *Rita Hayworth*
and *Shawshank Redemption*                             **34**
*Macbeth* and *Christine*                              **41**
Other Themes                                            47

**Chapter 3. The Masters' Early Influences** ...................51

Shakespeare's Influences                                58

**Chapter 4. Where Did They Get Their Inspiration?** ....67

King's Inspirations                                     73

**Chapter 5. Turning Points In Their Careers**.................81

King's Turning Points                                   87

**Chapter 6. Newsworthy Moments And Controversy**..93

Controversy and Stephen King                            98

Chapter 7. The Late And The Great ............................ 105

King's Legacy                                          110

Chapter 8. Major Successes, Relevance, And
Importance ................................................................ 113

Chapter 9. Ten Surprising Facts About William
Shakespeare ............................................................. 117

Chapter 10. Ten Surprising Facts About Stephen
King ............................................................................ 123

What's Next? ............................................................. 129

Endnotes .................................................................... 131

# CHAPTER 1.
## MASHUPS? WE BEGIN

Imagine this scene: A writer sits down to pen a tale centered around revenge, trickery, and the lobbing off of body parts to be served for dinner. Most of the characters have gone crazy and are preoccupied with killing one another. Now the question arises: Who is the author?

Maybe the first name you thought of was Stephen King, author of bestselling horror books like *Carrie*, *Christine*, and *The Shining*. But this plot is from English bard William Shakespeare, the king of the sonnet. And this particular scenario is from his sixteenth century play *Titus Andronicus*, in which Queen Tamora is tricked into eating her own sons. Their bodies have been hacked up and plated for her dinner.

Shakespeare is best known for his plays, ironic comedies and gripping tragedies. There's a lot of love, death, murder, insanity, and suicide in his works. Love and violence, paranoia and bloody killings also appear in many of King's novels. He's a master of horror.

Both authors highlight their views on humanity, praising the good at heart and punishing the wicked. Both invoke their own personal experiences, leaving autobiographical imprints on their fictional works. Elements such as childhood innocence, tragic heroism, isolation, and family struggles are common to both authors. Their works are immediate and accessible to readers of all ages.

While seemingly worlds and centuries apart, these two famous writers have a lot in common.

## Why Should You Care? Because Mashups Create More to Ponder and Tickle Your Brain!

The word "mashup" has been widely used over the past few decades. Historically speaking, the word was used by citizens of the British West Indies to refer to someone who was so intoxicated that he or she could not function properly. It was also used as a general description for an object that was not performing as constructed.

More recently, mashup has been defined as a musical phenomenon in which components of two or more songs are combined to create one song; this is a literal mashing together of the song samples.

The first song in history to be released in this category was the 1956 track "The Flying Saucer." It was put out by artists Bill Buchanan and Dickie Goodman. They classified it as a "break-in" song in reference to the parts of the song that "broke into" clips of completely different songs. However, Buchanan and Goodman were sued more than two dozen times for their illicit use of songs from other artists.

Fortunately, the judge presiding over the cases stated that Buchanan and Goodie had created a "burlesque," or a piece of new material that, although taken from the works of other artists, was entirely theirs. "Burlesques" are known today as mashups. They are protected under the United States Constitution.

Mashups are popular with DJs who have the freedom to create these mashed up tracks and use them as an expression of art.

The song "The Flying Saucer" eventually climbed the charts to the top ten in the United States. This was a testament to the popularity of mashups, and a good indication of the phenomenon they would become.[1]

The word mashup is also used nowadays to refer to web development. Typically, mashups are a web creation such as a page or an application that uses material from different sources to create an entirely new service.

For example, you might use a website that projected all of the different grocery stores in your area and superimpose that image over a Google Maps snapshot of another location to create a visual. This feature would take the one platform – the grocery store locator – and mash it up with Google Maps. That way you can pinpoint the most geographically near or distant grocery store.[2]

Mashup books take two or more characters or two or more events in history and combine them to formulate a completely different experience. This is not easy to do.

During the process of mashing together two or more songs, DJs and musicians commonly find either a beat or a word that can link things together. Therefore, there's a relevancy between the songs. Thus, the reason for their linkage might, after a few listens, become clear. Mashing up books, however, is often less straightforward. The mashups of two authors or concepts may be worlds, centuries, and genres apart. A deep look is required to see how some of the more profound elements, such as views on humanity and justice, are shared between the subjects in the mashup.

One of the most popular mashup books is the novel *Abraham Lincoln, Vampire Hunter* by Seth Grahame-Smith. Published in 2010, the book links the biography of Abraham Lincoln with the subject of vampires. The sixteenth president of the United States was not, of course, a vampire hunter. In fact, vampires are the creation of the Italian-English poet and physician John Polidori.

In 1918, Polidori published the short story "The Vampyre," which chronicles the mysterious Lord Ruthven, an attractive yet fear-provoking character.[3] The central character of the story would eventually morph into the vampires so popular today in books like *Twilight* and television series like *The Vampire Diaries*.

In Grahame-Smith's novel, a young Abe Lincoln finds out his grandfather was killed by a vampire and his mother died after succumbing to a fatal dose of vampire blood. These two events confirm for him the existence of vampires.

The future U.S. president writes in his diary that he will dedicate himself to slaying as many vampires as he possibly can. He later comes into contact with a slave owner who is a vampire. The slave owner uses his slaves to feed his need for blood. This causes Lincoln to become an avid abolitionist.

Throughout the novel, the character mentions other famous historical figures he thinks might be vampire hunters as well.

Grahame-Smith's novel was very well-received, garnering the following review in the *Los Angeles Times*:

"[A]t a time when the market is flooded with vampire titles, most of them young adult romances, a writer who can transform the greatest figure from 19th century American history into the star of an original vampire tale with humor, heart and bite is a rare find indeed."[4]

The novel was turned into a movie in 2012, directed by Timur Bekmambetov.[5]

Abraham Lincoln was reserved, wise, cunning, yet generous. The protagonist of Grahame-Smith's novel is the same kind of person, a man seeking to bring justice to his family name and abolish the evils that he sees (the vampire killers, the slave owners). The real Abe Lincoln was also striving to abolish evil in the form of slavery. Thus, the mashup with vampire stories serves as a way to project this historic figure in a new, but nevertheless heroic, light.

Other popular mashup novels include *Pride and Prejudice and Zombies*, also by Seth Grahame-Smith, *Sense and Sensibility and Sea Monsters* by Ben H. Winters, and *Little Women and Werewolves* by Porter Grand.[6]

William Shakespeare is known as one of history's greatest writers of English language works. He has also entered the stadium of mashup books. In 2014, popular author Christopher Moore published the novel *The Serpent of Venice*, with elements of Shakespeare's *The Merchant of Venice* and *Othello* coupled with Edgar Allan Poe's short story "The Cask of Amontillado." Moore's contemporary novel proves the work of Shakespeare is still accessible, and the situations and characters in his plays can still be transformed to fit any time period.[7]

Ian Doescher wrote a novel in which Shakespeare intersected with *Star Wars*. After gaining the necessary permissions, Doescher published *William Shakespeare's Star Wars: Verily, a New Hope* in 2013. The author remains faithful to the plot of the *Star Wars* movies while retelling the stories in Shakespearean language.

The Prologue of Doescher's epic mashup reads as follows:

> It is a period of civil war.
> The spaceships of the rebels, striking swift
> From base unseen, have gain'd a vict'ry o'er
> The cruel Galactic Empire, now adrift.
> Amidst the battle, rebel spies prevail'd
> And stole the plans to a space station vast,
> Whose pow'rful beams will later be unveil'd
> And crush a planet: 'tis the DEATH STAR blast.
> Pursu'd by agents sinister and cold,
> Now Princess Leia to her home doth flee,
> Deliv'ring plans and a new hope they hold:
> Of bringing freedom to the galaxy.

In time so long ago begins our play, In
star-crossed galaxy far, far away.[8]

The novel was received with such critical acclaim that it spawned a series; the sequel was entitled *William Shakespeare's The Empire Striketh Back*, and, later, *William Shakespeare's The Jedi Doth Return*.

There have also been mashups which used the works of Stephen King. In late 2012, the website, "Comics Should Be Good" posed a challenge to their followers to invent the best Stephen King/comic book mashups. They posted artwork that would go along with the comic books if they were published.

Some of the entries included "The Joker as It," "Mouse Guard and Pet Sematary," and "Scarecrow in Children of the Corn."[9]

Although the stories of Stephen King are typically horror with some aspects of science fiction, the author depicts more profound elements as well. He focuses on the triumph of good over evil, the innocence of a child's perspective, human suffering, teenage rebellion, and other themes of import. There have not been any mashups to date that center on the deeper facets of King's works; all of them focus solely on the fantastical and the horrific.

*Masters Mashup: From Shakespeare to Stephen King* brings to light elements that are shared between these two amazing authors. The focus is on their humanitarian views, notions of good versus evil, the inclusion of their own characteristics and personal histories in the characters they create, and the timelessness of both sets of works.

Throughout the following chapters, comparisons will be drawn by illustrating select works from each author. You will soon see how good old Shakespeare has more in common with twentieth century horror author Stephen King than most people think.

So, let's get thee hence with the first Mashup!

# CHAPTER 2.
# STEPHEN KING AND THE KING OF SONNETS: THE WORKS

Here's an odd coincidence: both writers are associated with towns named Stratford! Shakespeare's hometown is Stratford-upon-Avon, which is located in England. Stephen King spent part of his childhood living in Stratford, Connecticut.[10]

Both men also experienced much change in their early lives. William Shakespeare's father, John Shakespeare, frequently changed jobs beginning in the 1550s. At one point, he was the Stratford-upon-Avon taster of ale, meaning that he was employed to judge the quality of beer the borough produced! Just after his son was born, however, he lost most of their savings. Although John worked for a time as the mayor of Stratford, he and his wife could neither read nor write. Later, William's children were also unable to read or write.

No records exist to confirm the birth date of William Shakespeare, although the Holy Trinity Church in his hometown possesses documents showing that he was baptized on April 26, 1564. Today, the bard's birthday is celebrated on April 23rd. He is said to have been educated at the King's New School in Stratford. However, there is dispute as to whether or not Shakespeare was actually formally educated.

In fact, some believe Shakespeare did not exist, or if he did, he was not the author of the works attributed to him. Some think the former Earl of Oxford Edward De Vere was the author of the plays of Shakespeare.[11]

Between his teenage years and the first appearance of his work, little is known about the great Shakespeare. Records indicate he did get married, to Anne Hathaway, a woman eight years his senior who was already pregnant. Hathaway bore him a daughter, Susanna, and a set of twins, Hamnet and Judith.

After the twins were baptized, however, Shakespeare spent his time between 1585 and 1592 doing "next to nothing." Historians have speculated that he traveled and worked as a school teacher. He is also said to have spent much time away from his family, possibly in London in order to promote his plays and work with his actors. This is likely considering there are records of other poets and dramatists critiquing his work.[12]

In contrast, there is no question as to the authenticity of Stephen King's work. Nor is there any doubt regarding his identity. King was born on September 21, 1947. His father abandoned the family when the author was young and relocated to Fort Wayne, Indiana. His mother moved the family around the country, including for a time to Stratford, Connecticut, before finally settling in Durham, Maine.

King got his official start in writing when he was in college. He contributed a weekly column to the school newspaper. His professional breakthrough came before he turned twenty years old, so he was eight years younger than Shakespeare had been when he made his debut. King published his short story in 1967 in the magazine *Cemetery Dance*.[13]

"The Glass Floor" is a captivating mystery. Anthony Reynard has just lost his wife in a tragic accident when he visits his deceased wife's brother, Charles Wharton. In speaking about her death, Reynard claims that Janine fell off a ladder while dusting a bookshelf in their library. The peculiar room has a floor made entirely out of glass which acts as a mirror. Reynard says his wife slipped from the ladder and broke her neck. The details of the incident leave Wharton wanting to know more about his sister's demise.

Critics have pointed to King's naiveté as a young author, stating that his writing style contained an abundance of adverbs. King has long advised new writers to avoid falling into the trap of adverb overuse. However, the story provides the plot twists and the highly developed characters King would later become known for. He sold the story to *Cemetery Dance* for thirty-five dollars.[14]

In comparison to what he would be making years down the road, this meager check was not much pay. But King continued to write out of sheer passion for the work and a genuine desire to tell a good story.

Like Shakespeare, King also worked for a time as a teacher. He taught English at Hampden Academy, a high school in Maine. Teaching allowed him to work on the academic schedule so he had enough time to write.

Shakespeare wrote to survive, as he did not want to fall into the same cycle of debt as his father. Still, he exhibited the same ardor for story-telling as King does today.

The two authors' works share the element of humanity. Their characters are human and fallible, so real they are completely accessible to global audiences. The two authors' plots are appealing and provide enough of a hook to keep readers turning pages. Their aim is to get at the heart of the reader's emotions and provide a powerful story.

Take a look at the following comparisons between the two authors' works. You will be able to see the many similarities between Stephen King and the King of the Sonnet.

### *Titus Andronicus* and *Carrie*

The first theme is revenge. A common element in many of King's novels, revenge is also the centerpiece for Shakespeare's *Titus Andronicus*. The story is bloody, painfully violent, and full of rage; these are the same elements Stephen King included in his novel *Carrie*.

*Titus Andronicus* is said to have been written in the early 1590s. The play opens after the death of the Roman Emperor. His sons Saturninus and Bassianus are fighting over who will take charge of the empire. The Roman people, however, favor the warrior hero Titus Andronicus.

Titus Andronicus has spent a decade fighting the Goths, and he has captured their Queen, Tamora. He's also captured her sons Alarbus, Demetrius, and Chironas, well as a Moor named Aaron. Titus Andronicus kills Queen Tamora's son Alarbus, claiming his act as an even exchange for *his* sons lost in the war.

After this spectacle, there is much hope that war hero Titus Andronicus will ascend to the throne and rule the empire with his valor and cunning. He, however, makes known his support for Saturninus for emperor instead.

Emperor Saturninus tells Titus that his first order of business is to marry his daughter Lavinia. However, she is engaged to Bassianus.

Thus, the plan does not sit well with Bassianus and the two brothers begin to quarrel. In the midst of the family feud, the Moor Aaron convinces Tamora's remaining sons to kill Bassianus and rape Lavinia. They do so and, in order to keep Lavinia quiet, they cut out her tongue. They also chop off her hands. Then Aaron forges a letter to pin the murder of Bassianus on Titus's other two sons. The young men's heads are cut off and sent to their father, which causes him to go crazy.

Tamora takes advantage of Titus's insanity. She goes to him dressed as Revenge, with her sons in tow dressed as Murder and Rape. When Revenge (Tamora) leaves Titus's house, he murders her two sons, drains the blood from their slit throats, and promises his daughter that he will cook the boys' bodies for the following night's feast.

The next day, Titus convinces himself that he cannot have a daughter who has been violated. He kills Lavinia in yet another act of insanity.

When Tamora comes to dinner, he serves her a meal that has been prepared with the bodies of her sons. After she finishes eating, he tells her she has just eaten her sons, then kills her.

Emperor Saturninus murders Titus before he is killed himself by Lucius, Titus's only remaining son. Aaron is sentenced to be buried alive so that he will die of starvation or thirst.

The play is divided into fourteen scenes over five acts. During this time, the author manages to kill fourteen characters in a series of gruesome events. The horror in this play is the exact sort of entertainment audiences of the time craved. Shakespeare gave the people what they wanted to see. Many theatre goers could not wait to see the newest gory tragedy, and *Titus Andronicus*, without a doubt, fits that profile.[15]

Centuries later, the same type of gruesome tale centered on cold-blooded revenge was written by Stephen King. *Carrie* was published in 1974, almost four hundred years after *Titus Andronicus*.

High school student Carrie is living in a confusing world. She's being raised by a single mother who is bizarrely religious and frequently behaves in a manic manner. To make matters worse, Carrie is an outcast:

> Carrie stood among them stolidly, a frog among
> swans. She was a chunky girl with pimples on
> her neck and back and buttocks, her wet hair
> completely without color. It rested against her face
> with dispirited sogginess and she simply stood,
> head slightly bent, letting the water splat against
> her flesh and roll off. She looked the part of the
> sacrificial goat, the constant butt, believer in left-
> handed monkey wrenches, perpetual foul-up,
> and she was. She wished forlornly and constantly
> that Ewen High had individual—and thus private—
> showers, like the high schools at Westover or
> Lewiston. They stared. They always stared.[16]

Carrie gets her period for the first time in the shower after gym class. The girls in the locker room make fun of her. When a light bulb in the bathroom blows up, this demonstrates Carrie's telekinetic abilities. One girl, Chris, gets in trouble.

Sue sympathizes with Carrie. She convinces her boyfriend Tommy to take Carrie to the prom. When Chris finds out, she convinces *her* boyfriend Billy to plot against Carrie. Billy slays two pigs, drains their blood into buckets, and sets up the buckets at the prom.

When Carrie and Tommy are announced as the prom king and queen, the buckets are tipped, showering the two with pigs' blood. Tommy dies from being hit in the head with the bucket.

Amidst the ensuing chaos, Carrie uses her telekinetic powers to lock the gym doors and set the gym on fire, burning everyone inside. Carrie walks home. Her mother confesses that she was raped and Carrie was the byproduct. Then she stabs her daughter. Carrie again uses her mind powers, this time to stop her mother's heart. She later kills Chris and Billy by telepathically controlling their car and crashing it.

Sue sees Carrie fall to the ground after killing all her tormentors. Sue rushes over and Carrie dies in her arms. Due to this telepathic exposure, Sue loses the baby she was carrying, Tommy's child.

The "Black Prom" has claimed the lives of nearly five hundred people.

There are three main themes shared by *Titus Andronicus* and *Carrie*. The first is violence against and manipulation of female characters, which provides the catalyst for widespread killing. Lavinia and Carrie's mother are the victims of rape, an act which would later cause both of their deaths.

Lavinia and Carrie are silenced and taken advantage of. Lavinia is literally silenced when her tongue is cut out, preventing her from identifying her rapists. She is also figuratively silenced in that she has no choice as to the outcome of her marital life. In fact, two men fight over her hand in marriage as though it were a commodity.

Carrie too experiences silencing due to her social positioning at school. She is an outcast and therefore voiceless at her high school. Her mother sheltered her from the facts of life for religious reasons, but this meant that Carrie was silenced regarding her own womanhood. Carrie can only "speak" and regain control of her life by using the powers of her mind.

The second common theme is revenge. A desire for revenge is apparent in many of the characters' motives in *Titus Andronicus*. Titus seeks to avenge the memory of his sons and, in doing so, kills one of Queen Tamora's boys. Tamora gets back at Titus by visiting him dressed as Revenge. Titus seeks revenge for the atrocities committed against his daughter by killing her other two sons.

No wonder *Titus Andronicus* is known as one of Shakespeare's "revenge tragedies."

In *Carrie*, the protagonist is picked on by the other girls, and one gets in trouble. Chris then seeks revenge, using her boyfriend to come up with the prom plot. Carrie, in turn, kills all the students at the prom as she seeks revenge on the institution that has alienated her. Her mother's attempt to kill her was also a plot of revenge, one against the daughter who served as a reminder of a long-ago rape.

The third theme the two works share is deception. Titus is duped into believing his own sons murdered Bassianus and raped Lavinia. Queen Tamora is tricked into eating her sons. She fools Titus by posing as Revenge.

Carrie is deceived during her date to the prom. She has no idea she will be humiliated in front of her classmates. She does not know that she was elected prom queen after Chris had her friends fill the ballot box with Carrie's name.

One other thing the two works have in common is the inclusion of a supporting character who serves to aid the others in their endeavors. Aaron in *Titus Andronicus* and Sue in *Carrie* deliver assistance, moving the plot forward. Aaron comes up with the plan to have Bassianus killed; Sue convinces her boyfriend to elevate Carrie's social status by taking her to the prom. Both supporting characters are not rewarded for their actions. Aaron is buried alive and Sue suffers a miscarriage.

Coincidentally, the first on-stage musical production of *Carrie* was in 1988 by the Royal Shakespeare Company in Stratford-upon-Avon.

Later, the musical went to Broadway.

### *Hamlet* and *The Shining*

Two other works of notable similarity are Shakespeare's *Hamlet* and King's *The Shining*. The two works focus on father-son relationships, insanity, guilt, and piety, and both include ghosts.

*Hamlet* is Shakespeare's longest play and, like *The Shining*, it is a twisted tragedy. In the opening of the play, the Prince of Hamlet has recently lost his father, the King of Denmark. Prince Hamlet is also the nephew of King Claudius, who is in line to take the throne. In accepting his kingly duties, Claudius marries Hamlet's mother, Gertrude.

Other characters talk about the appearance of a strange ghost that resembles the recently deceased King. Though they try to engage the ghost in conversation, they are unsuccessful. Their stories are told to the Prince.

This is all the Prince needs to hear. He has already been behaving in a crazed manner, as he is depressed over his father's death. Here is his famous soliloquy:

> O that this too too solid flesh would melt,
> Thaw, and resolve itself into a dew!
> Or that the Everlasting had not fix'd
> His canon 'gainst self-slaughter! O God! God!
> How weary, stale, flat, and unprofitable
> Seem to me all the uses of this world!

In this passage, he says the world is useless to him. This monologue evidences the beginnings of what would advance to a deeply insane state.

Hamlet chastises his mother for jumping into bed with and marrying King Claudius so soon after her husband died. Prince Hamlet is visited by the ghost of his father, who tells him that it was Claudius who killed him and that his death must now be avenged.

Prince Hamlet agrees that something must be done about Claudius, but he is not certain he trusts the ghost. He acts manic afterward, and this upsets his lover, Ophelia. When she disapproves of his behavior, he commands that she be sent to a nunnery. Once again, there is the silencing and the powerlessness of a woman in a Shakespeare play.

Hamlet decides to put on a play for the family in which he will act out his father's murder. He figures he will be able to see how Claudius reacts to the scene and then know whether his uncle killed his father.

During the play's murder scene, Claudius rises from his seat and leaves. This is enough evidence for Prince Hamlet to seek revenge on his uncle.

Hamlet is soon presented with the opportunity to kill Claudius while his uncle is praying. Instead, he unintentionally kills Polonius, Ophelia's father, who had been spying on the prince and his mother. Ophelia then drowns herself.

Claudius devises a plan with Laertes, Ophelia's brother. Laertes will challenge Hamlet to a fencing match, but will use a rapier dipped in poison. However, Hamlet kills Laertes. Then he kills Claudius.

As in *Titus Andronicus*, a handful of characters in *Hamlet* are killed due to insanity and the insane desire for revenge.

The main character in Stephen King's novel *The Shining* also goes mad. Jack Torrance, like Hamlet, destroys his family due to his hallucinations and his insane rage.

It is interesting to note that King has admitted he used his own struggles while creating the character of Jack Torrance. Jack is said to be King's most autobiographical character. Both went through a period of heavy drinking. King's heaviest drug and alcohol use occurred during the 1980s.[17]

King has stated that his character in *The Shining* was fighting off internal and external demons. Like Hamlet, Jack Torrance made decisions influenced by the demons that had appeared in his life and in his own mind, demons he had tried desperately to rid himself of.

In *The Shining*, Jack, his wife Wendy, and their son Danny move into the Overlook Hotel. Jack has been hired to look after the mountaintop vacation spot during the long cold winter when all access roads are closed. Jack takes the job in order to do right by his family, who he has harmed in the past on violent alcoholic binges. In fact, he once broke his young son's arm.

Wendy had decided not to leave her husband because Danny loves him. However, Danny is fearful that his mother and father will split up:

> The greatest terror of Danny's life was DIVORCE,
> a word that always appeared in his mind
> as a sign painted in red letters which were
> covered in hissing, poisonous snakes.

Danny has other terrifying thoughts. Not long after arriving at Overlook Hotel, he realizes that he has premonitions and knows what other people are thinking. He also sees apparitions, ghosts that appear to him around the hotel. These ghosts become increasingly frightening, but he does not tell his parents; he is more concerned about his father keeping his job as caretaker. The spirits become hostile, eventually preying on Jack.

One night, Jack goes down to the hotel bar. He sees that it is stocked with alcohol. Before, the shelves had been empty.

Jack meets a ghost bartender who persuades him to drink, and then to kill Wendy and Danny. Jack's violent rampage begins as he pursues his wife and son. Displaying disturbing honesty, Jack calls to his wife, "Wendy? Darling? Light, of my life. I'm not gonna hurt ya. I'm just going to bash your brains in."

Despite Wendy's attempts to escape, Jack continues to pursue her before setting his sights on Danny. In a moment of clarity, however, Jack's violent spell subsides and he tells his son to run away. Danny and Wendy manage to escape right before the boiler in the basement of the Overlook Hotel explodes. Jack is killed.

There are three themes that link these works. Insanity is one. *Hamlet* features a young man who plans to go insane; he confesses that he will adopt an "antic disposition" in order to confuse King Claudius. He successfully adopts manic behaviors to trick his family and friends into thinking he has lost his mind. Is he really insane? This is hotly debated in literary circles.

Jack Torrance *is* insane, possibly possessed by the spirits of the Overlook Hotel. There is no question about Jack's insanity; he loses his mind and only seems to gain mental clarity when he realizes the danger he poses to his own son.

Another theme in both works is a distortion of reality. In each, the main character is acting upon mysterious forces that have apparently possessed him. Hamlet is convinced to kill Claudius by a ghost that claims to be his father. Jack is overtaken, mentally and physically, by the ghosts that haunt the Overlook Hotel.

*The Shining* displays other elements that are supernatural. For example, plants take shape and move around the hotel property. And the novel includes a child with supernatural powers, an element that is absent from Shakespeare's work. King often uses children in his stories. Carrie and Danny both have special mental powers.

Family is a third theme in the two works. Hamlet is loyal to his father, willing to do whatever it takes to avenge his death. Jack's son is self-sacrificing, remaining in danger in order to help his father keep the job at the hotel.

The impetus behind the authors' use of family strife might have been the relationships they experienced in their own families. Shakespeare lost his son Hamnet when the boy was eleven. Thus, *Hamlet* is thought to be a biographical work examining the loss. King was abandoned by his father; the way Jack hurts Danny could be interpreted as the kind of pain a boy feels when his father deserts the family.

Whatever the impetus for writing these works, the similarities are there, and both storylines provide for memorable reading experiences.

### *Richard III* and *Rita Hayworth and Shawshank Redemption*

Loneliness and isolation are two elements explored in both the plays of William Shakespeare and the fiction of Stephen King. In the works of these authors, characters are often isolated, tragic, and somewhat heroic.

Two good examples of this are Shakespeare's *Richard III* and King's *Rita Hayworth and Shawshank Redemption*, which became the popular film *The Shawshank Redemption*.

Believed to have been written in 1592, *Richard III* details the reign of King Richard III of England. In the play, Richard is an ugly, deformed outcast who vows he will become a villain and engage in deceptive behaviors.

First on his list is duping Lady Anne to marry him, even though he plans to get rid of her later. Second, he turns the court against him, including the nobles and the widow of the recently deceased Henry VI. Next, Richard has his brother murdered because Clarence is first in line to inherit the throne. Richard then informs his other brother, Edward IV, that Clarence has died. This causes Edward so much grief that he dies.

Richard then proceeds to have everyone killed off who stands in the way of his ascension to the throne. He poisons Lady Anne so he can pursue Elizabeth of York, the daughter of Queen Elizabeth.

Then a battle breaks out between Richard and the people who were once his closest allies. On the night before the battle, he sees the ghosts of the people he has had killed. He awakens with the realization that every person in his life has turned against him; he can no longer depend on anyone, not even himself.

Here is a famous passage from the play that illustrates just how alone and isolated Richard feels in the wake of his manipulative and selfish actions:

> Give me another horse! Bind up my wounds!
> Have mercy, Jesu!—Soft, I did but dream.
> O coward conscience, how dost thou afflict me!
> The lights burn blue. It is now dead midnight.
> Cold fearful drops stand on my trembling flesh.
> What do I fear? Myself? There's none else by.
> Richard loves Richard; that is, I and I.
> Is there a murderer here? No. Yes, I am.
> Then fly! What, from myself? Great reason why:

Lest I revenge. What, myself upon myself?
Alack, I love myself. Wherefore? For any good
That I myself have done unto myself?
O, no! Alas, I rather hate myself
For hateful deeds committed by myself.
I am a villain. Yet I lie. I am not.
Fool, of thyself speak well. Fool, do not flatter.[18]

In this telling section, he realizes that he has no one to blame but himself, that he has no one to fear but himself, and that he is a murderer, for which he begins to hate himself. He confesses, "I am a villain."

Richard meets his fate during the battle. He is killed. The princess Elizabeth of York marries the man who killed Richard.

Isolation and confinement are also explored in Stephen King's *Rita Hayworth and Shawshank Redemption*. The plot centers around banker Andy Dufresne, who is found guilty of killing his wife and her lover. Andy is sentenced to life in Shawshank Prison. There he befriends an inmate named Red who is able to get anything a man needs from the outside world.

Andy collects rocks and he asks Red to procure a rock hammer from the outside. He also asks Red for a poster of then-popular actress Rita Hayworth. Later, Red gets him posters of other actresses like Marilyn Monroe. Andy hangs these on the wall of his cell.

Andy needs protection against an inmate gang known as The Sisters, so he helps out a guard who is struggling with a heavy tax burden. Andy advises him on how to deal with a large inheritance and avoid paying the tax.

He has thereby proven his usefulness to the warden, so Andy is permitted a single cell. He is also allowed to work in the prison library. When he writes to the Senate for extra funding to beef up the scant collection of books, they receive monies. He also manages to obtain more books for the library, including references he can use to help inmates earn diplomas. Andy is a heroic figure.

Eighteen years pass by. One day Andy confesses to Red that he has money in bank accounts under the name Peter Stevens. He says he plans to relocate to Mexico and purchase property.

Nearly a decade after this revelation, Andy disappears from his cell. He had carved out a tunnel, which he kept hidden behind the posters Red got him. This carving process had been done slowly and over a long period of time in order to not attract attention from the guards.

When Red receives an unsigned postcard from Texas, he assumes Andy has made it to Mexico. After Red is released from prison, he follows the directions Andy gave him to a small town in Maine. There he finds a note hidden in a rock wall. The note instructs Red to go to Mexico. There is also cash. The note is signed "Peter Stevens."

Richard III and Andy Dufresne display some similar characteristics. The first shared theme is the fall from grace. Richard III, a social outcast, manages to win the promise of marrying Lady Anne and ascending to the throne to become King. He then chooses to eliminate all the people who stand in his way. So it is his own selfishness that causes him to fall from the temporary grace he had achieved.

Andy, on the other hand, begins his story with a fall from grace, after being convicted of a double murder. He then uses the people around him to his own advantage in order to ensure his ascension. His ascension is not to a throne but out of prison.

Richard falls deeper and deeper into despair with every person he kills, until he himself is killed. Andy begins at the bottom rung in the prison ladder, working his way up until he finally gets his freedom.

The second theme linking the two works is manipulation and cunning. Both protagonists are astute enough to size up the attributes of the people around them in order to successfully use them for their own purposes.

Richard was able to make Lady Anne fall in love with him, thereby inflating his own stature. He was then able to manipulate the normal order of ascension to the throne with his murderous skills.

Andy, on the other hand, was able to determine what qualities about each person in his life could be most useful to him. While human emotion becomes an obstacle in *Richard III*, as Richard's fear of his adversaries leads to his demise, Andy is always calm and reserved when interacting with the inmates and the guards. In this way, he able to maintain the mental clarity required while he manipulates the other prisoners, the guards, even the warden.

The third theme is that of isolation and solitude. In *Richard III*, the protagonist is intensely aware of his own folly, and he knows that his own actions will inevitably bring him pain. It is through his dreams and the visitation from the ghosts that he realizes he is alone in the world. While not a standard hero, Richard embodies all of the negative qualities of the tragic hero. These include inner dialogue, self-reflection, and self-inflicted suffering.

Andy is physically and mentally isolated. He is bound by the bars of his cell, the walls of the prison, and the barriers around the property that keep the inmates trapped. Red explains the human desire to want to be free from bondage:

> "Some birds are not meant to be caged, that's all. Their feathers are too bright, their songs too sweet and wild. So you let them go, or when you open the cage to feed them they somehow fly out past you. And the part of you that knows it was wrong to imprison them in the first place rejoices, but still, the place where you live is that much more drab and empty for their departure."

Andy is further isolated in a single cell where, like Richard, he is able to reflect, and to devise his plan. Andy acts in solitude; he digs himself out of his cell by himself, without divulging his escape plan to anyone else. He makes sure that he has the proper materials, which he secures for himself by manipulating those around him.

He is the hero of his own story, as he helps the other prisoners, including Red. And he successfully ensures his own escape.

Richard III and Andy Dufresne illustrate how we might experience a fall from grace. There is the possibility for redemption, but not all of us choose that path.

## *Macbeth* and *Christine*

*Macbeth* is believed to have been written by Shakespeare between 1599 and 1606, and the play was first performed in 1606.[19] *Christine* was published in 1983. The two works seem quite different, but they share themes including vanity, excessive use of power, and the interference of supernatural and possessive spirits.

When the play opens, Macbeth and Banquo have won a battle for Scotland against Norway and Ireland. Three Witches appear. They praise Macbeth, informing him that he will eventually become king. They tell Banquo that members of his lineage will also become king, but he himself will never bear that title.

Macbeth is soon named the Thane of Cawdor, and he begins to speculate whether the Witches prophecies will come true. However, the current King has named his son Malcolm, not Macbeth, as next in line for the throne.

Lady Macbeth advises her husband to kill King Duncan. So Macbeth and his wife get the King's chamberlains drunk, then sneak into his chamber while he is asleep. Macbeth cannot go through with the murder, but Lady Macbeth stabs the King. King Duncan's sons Malcolm and Donalbain escape to other countries to avoid being killed themselves.

Since they have fled, the sons are suspects in the king's murder, leaving the path to the throne open to Macbeth. He is crowned the new King of Scotland.

Remembering the prediction of the Three Witches that Banquo was father of a line of kings, Macbeth plans to have him and his son Fleance killed. Banquo is killed but Fleance escapes.

Later, at a banquet, the ghost of Banquo appears. But Macbeth is the only person in the room who can see the apparition. Lady Macbeth sends the guests home.

Macbeth tracks down the Three Witches and they confirm that, for now, he is safe. However, they tell him he will be defeated by someone who is not "of woman born" and Banquo's lineage will in fact breed a line of kings in many countries.

While Macbeth feels more secure about his fate since *all* people are born of women, his wife's guilt is slowly driving her insane. She imagines she can see bloodstains on her hands.

She eventually kills herself. Others are intent on seeking revenge by killing Macbeth. These events culminate in Macbeth's famous soliloquy:

> Tomorrow, and tomorrow, and tomorrow,
> Creeps in this petty pace from day to day,
> To the last syllable of recorded time;

And all our yesterdays have lighted fools
The way to dusty death. Out, out, brief candle!
Life's but a walking shadow, a poor player,
That struts and frets his hour upon the stage,
And then is heard no more. It is a tale
Told by an idiot, full of sound and fury,
Signifying nothing.[20]

Macbeth realizes there is a futility to his life. After Macduff beheads Macbeth, he makes it known he was born by Caesarean section. This brings the Three Witches' prophecy to fruition since Macduff was not born in the natural sense.

King Duncan's son Malcolm returns to become the next King of Scotland.

Like some of the other tragic characters in Shakespeare's repertoire, Macbeth falls victim to his own selfishness. He tries to overrule the premonition of the Three Witches who have told him of the obstacles to his ambition. He is so focused on ascending to the throne that he eliminates all the people who stand in his way. His vanity and thirst for power are what lead to his demise.

Vanity and power also come into play in King's novel *Christine*, which tells the story of a rogue car. This supernatural car impacts the life of those who come in contact with it.

The story opens with teenager Arnie Cunningham driving around one day with his friend Dennis. When Arnie sees a 1958 Plymouth Fury for sale in front of a house, he purchases it from the owner, Roland D. LeBay.

When Dennis sits in the car, which is named Christine, he experiences disturbing flashbacks.

Arnie takes the car to an auto body shop. While Christine is being repaired, Arnie's character begins to change. He becomes an introvert but his self-esteem strengthens in direct proportion to his new detachment from others.

Dennis notices the changes that are taking place. When Roland passes away, Dennis decides to speak to the man's son. George LeBay tells Dennis that his father had bouts of violent behavior while the car was in his care. He also says two deaths occurred in the car; Roland's young daughter choked to death in the back seat, and Roland's wife was so overcome with grief she killed herself, also in the car.

Dennis finds out that Arnie is helping the auto body shop owner in illegal activities. He has become an entirely different person. Meanwhile, his popularity has increased because the most attractive girl in school has taken an interest in him.

Arnie picks up Leigh for a date in his new car. She chokes on a hamburger and almost dies. Arnie is useless and the girl is saved by a hitchhiker.

Christine is a sentient being, jealous of anyone Arnie devotes his time to, including Leigh.

Leigh is aware of the fact that the car appears to be vying for Arnie's attention and she decides to never sit in it again. Arnie's father also sees the problems the car is creating and takes it away from his son. While parked out in a lot, some kids from Arnie's school smash up the car. When Arnie repairs the car, the kids who trashed it die in mysterious ways.

Although the police are able to connect Christine to the various deaths, there is no physical proof that the car was actually present when the accidents took place.

The connections between the car, Arnie, and Roland LeBay become clear when Dennis talks to Leigh. They conclude that Christine has taken on Roland's violent personality, and agree the killing needs to stop. While Arnie is away, his two friends put the car through a crusher.

Christine is smushed, but the spirit of Roland escapes from the car. The enraged apparition is then responsible for the death of Arnie, his mother, and his father.

Years later, Dennis is working as a teacher. When he hears about an accident in Los Angeles he immediately knows it was caused by Christine. He fears that the car has rebuilt itself and will come back for him.

The themes shared by *Macbeth* and *Christine* are clear. However, readers need to look carefully to see how they mash up.

Macbeth is so absorbed with the idea of becoming king that he overlooks other aspects of the prophecy of the Three Witches. He destroys all his relationships when he goes on a killing spree to make sure he secures his spot on the throne.

Similarly, the vanity of owning a car like Christine changes Arnie, who becomes withdrawn yet obscenely self-assured. The teen does not realize his obsession with his car is hurting his relationships with the people around him.

Macbeth will do anything to become king, while Christine (or the spirit of the previous owner) is an all-powerful entity that seeks to control the car's owner. Arnie, in turn, finds himself feeling powerful when he owns the car. His obsession with the car clouds his ability to reason. He is possessed by the powers of the car and anyone who interferes is harmed or killed.

In both works, supernatural evil forces influence the lives and deaths of the main characters. Christine's evil spirits possess Arnie, while Macbeth makes choices based on his interactions with the Three Witches and the ghost of Banquo.

## Other Themes

Teenage rebellion is a theme that comes up many times in the works of both Shakespeare and King.

In *Romeo & Juliet*, two feuding families have been at war so long they are unable to recall what they are fighting over. Yet, in the keeping to their principles, the Montagues and the Capulets encourage their children to continue the antipathy.

In essence, the families are fighting for the sake of fighting, and sticking to tradition instead of striving to find a solution to their divisions. The play clearly displays the futility of remaining stagnant, refusing to embrace change. The play illustrates the harm done to generations bred in the midst of senseless and ongoing prejudice.

It is the teenage lovers Romeo and Juliet who must provide the catalyst for change. Unfortunately, it is through tragedy that their parents finally come to understand the ignorance and dangers inherent in their long held tradition.

Another theme of the play is teenage love and teenage rebellion. The young Romeo and Juliet defy their parents' wishes, rebelling against the restrictions placed upon them and expressing instead their feelings for one another. Here is Juliet's monologue on her balcony:

> O Romeo, Romeo! Wherefore art thou Romeo! Deny thy father and refuse thy name.
> Or, if thou wilt not, be but sworn my love, And I'll no longer be a Capulet.

This is one of the most famous scenes in Shakespeare's work. Juliet is well aware of the reasons why she cannot be with Romeo; she knows these are foolish. So she is encouraging them to cast aside the names that are the source of the feuding.

*Romeo & Juliet* remains accessible to today's readers who understand the emotions, who can relate to the adolescent pursuit of love despite a parent's scorn.

At the tragic end of the play, the audience sides with the young, dead lovers. Everyone feels contempt for parents blinded by tradition to the fatal effect that can have on their children.

Teenage rebellion was also explored in King's novel *Rage*. He wrote the book when he was in high school. The story focuses on a student who shoots his teacher and holds his classmates hostage.

*Rage* was taken out of print after several instances in which students brought guns to school, shot teachers, or held classmates hostage and claimed they were inspired by Stephen King's story.[21]

# CHAPTER 3.
# THE MASTERS' EARLY INFLUENCES

Stephen King experienced two events when he was a young boy that haunted him. These childhood traumas affected his life. They also influenced his writing.

Donald King, Stephen's father, earned a living as a vacuum salesman. He was also a womanizer who deserted his family in 1949. King has described this event as a classic tale of abandonment. His father walked out of the house, saying he was going to the grocery store to buy cigarettes, and he never returned. Stephen was only two years old at the time, but the effect his father's sudden departure had on him would be long lasting.[22]

The absence of his father would eventually come into play in his work. Years later, he claimed he would occasionally find himself missing the man. He confessed he used the twisted worlds of horror stories to forget about the abandonment he was forced to overcome.[23]

The second event occurred when King was a toddler.

The incident happened when he left his house to play with another little boy in the neighborhood. A few hours later, he came home alone. He was pale and upset, and he refused to speak.

His mother was worried and suspected something traumatic had happened to him. She also wondered why the mother of the other little boy had not escorted her son back to the house.

Mrs. King soon discovered the boy her son had been playing with had been hit and killed by a freight train.

King says he does not remember witnessing the event. He claims he only knows about it because he was informed years later that it happened. Deaths associated with trains, however, have been featured in some of his novels.[24]

In the years following these two events, King had nightmares in which his mother was dead or he was executed by hanging. The elements of horror stories were in his dreams: coffins, crows, clowns, gallows, and other subjects classic to the genre.

Young Stephen kept himself in a constant state of fear. He was afraid of the boogeyman, in those days an imaginary figure who haunted children's closets and dreams. Yet, he would secretly listen to the radio show *Dimension X*, scaring himself even more with the stories that were broadcast. Authors featured on the show included Ray Bradbury and Isaac Asimov.[25]

As a boy he had tonsillitis and other infections that forced him to remain in bed. To keep occupied, he read comic books. His mother worked different jobs to support Stephen and his brother. However, she shared with her children a love of reading, and this blossomed in her son Stephen during his bedridden period.

King took to devising his own versions of the comic book stories he read. When he showed what he had written to his mother, she encouraged him to write a story of his own. He invented a tale of a rabbit that could operate a car. His mother told him it was good enough to be a book.

Sometime later, King found a book his mother had borrowed from the library, *The Strange Case of Dr. Jekyll and Mr. Hyde* by Robert Louis Stevenson. Even though she had reservations about sharing the story with her timid son, she read it to him. He was mesmerized. The story cultivated an instant love for the element of horror, the concept of the split personality, and other dark aspects abundant in the novel.[26]

King's mother was also a fan of horror novels. Soon enough, the two began to share a passion for the books in that genre.

That same year, she took him to see the 1954 film *The Creature from the Black Lagoon*. The movie is about a group of scientists who venture into a part of the Amazon, the "black lagoon," in an attempt to find a gilled creature. They plan to capture it and take it back to the lab to study it.

The creature watches the scientists' arrival and stalks them. When it sees the beautiful female scientist, Kay Lawrence, it kidnaps her. After her colleagues rescue her, they shoot the creature.

Although King was only seven years old at the time , he remembered the entire movie vividly for years. In fact, seeing the movie taught him that he was able to hold images in his mind for a long time.

His photographic memory would serve him well later in life. All he had to do was take a mental snapshot of something, store it away for eventual use, then recall it when he sat down to write. Indeed, King is recognized for being able to seamlessly fuse two totally different concepts he has seen or experienced in order to create the plots for his novels.

While the elements in the film no doubt inspired him, his introduction to the world of horror mixed with science fiction solidified a few years later. When the family moved to Maine to live with his grandparents,

Stephen and his brother David found a box of their father's belongings. In the box was a book that would change Stephen King's life forever.

*The Lurker of the Threshold* was by H.P. Lovecraft, the author of tales about a character named Cthulhu. King devoured the collection. He later claimed it was the pivotal work in determining his future as a novelist.

It is ironic, however, that the young King took to the book so quickly. After all, it had belonged to his absentee father. But in this way, Donald King managed to influence his son. While the book by no means filled the void, it was fateful that his son stumbled on the book and drew inspiration from it that changed his life.

Another influence on Stephen King was Richard Matheson, the author of many haunting science fiction works including the 1954 novel *I Am Legend*. In this tale, Earth's population is made up of vampires with the exception of one man. Matheson also penned the 1956 novel *The Shrinking Man*, in which the main character does just what the title suggests.[27]

These fantastical, horrific novels lit the spark for young King, inspiring him to write his own horror stories. In terms of story construction, there have been similarities noted between the works of King and Matheson. Matheson wrote mostly in the third person with casual inclusion of the characters' internal thoughts and musings. King tends to do the same.

King was also inspired by how much he could relate to the horror stories that Matheson wrote because the tales unfolded in such common places. King said later:

> "It wasn't Eastern Europe — the horror could be in the 7-Eleven store down the block, or it could be just up the street. Something terrible could be going on even in a G.I. Bill-type ranch development near a college, it could be there as well. And to me, as a kid, that was a revelation, that was extremely exciting. He was putting the horror in places that I could relate to."[28]

The idea that the most horrific stories could take place in everyday locations appears many times in King's stories. He frequently uses real characters and events based loosely on people he knew or places he has visited. Readers are able to imagine these people and places because they are so real.

This is the same experience King had whenever he read Matheson's stories.

Reading and writing horror stories became a way for young Stephen King to protect himself from nightmares. He discovered he could control his fearful dreams and keep his deepest fears at bay if he buried himself in scary stories.

By the time he was a young man, all of the pieces had been set in place. King could draw on his literary and cinematic influences, as well as his photographic memory of scenes he had experienced. Soon he would learn to craft his own twisted stories for publication.

King officially kicked off his career as a writer in 1959 when he began writing articles for his brother David's newspaper. Known as *Dave's Rag*, the paper was a local publication the boys distributed themselves. Two stories that appeared have since gained attention. "Jumper" chronicles the attempt of a police officer trying to lure a man off of a ledge. The jumper is poised, all ready to fall to his death. The second story is about a team of doctors. There is little description in the stories and no plot twists. Instead, King focused on a single issue that readers could become immersed in.[29]

A few years later, King's stories were self-published in a collection known as "People, Place, and Things: Volume I." The collection featured stories with titles like "The Thing at the Bottom of the Well," "The Stranger," and "Hotel at the End of the Road."

In 1965, his story "I Was a Teenage Grave Robber" appeared in *Comics Review* magazine. King was still in high school. However, it was not until he published the novel *Carrie* almost a decade later that he came to the attention of the reading public.

## Shakespeare's Influences

Like Stephen King, William Shakespeare had many cultural, artistic, and literary influences. In the early 1590s, he was writing plays and acting in London. As a newcomer, he was desperate to make a name for himself. He worked hard to compete with the prominent artists of the time. These included Christopher Marlowe, a popular poet, playwright, and translator. Marlowe is said to have had a great influence on the young Shakespeare.

Although there are no documents proving the two ever met, there is much evidence that Shakespeare tried to compete with the other playwright. It could not have been easy for him. Marlowe had been educated at Corpus Christi College of Cambridge, while Shakespeare attended school only until the age of fifteen. Marlowe had translated many notable works and spoke various languages because he had traveled extensively. Shakespeare knew only English and had never left his home country. Marlowe was worldly and knew much about politics. All this has contributed to the speculation that Marlowe may be the real author of various Shakespearean works.[30]

There are many similarities between Marlowe's and Shakespeare's plays. Blank verse was a poetic writing style used by Marlowe in his plays *Dr. Faustus*, *Edward II*, *Dido of Queen Carthage*, and others. Blank verse is characterized by a likeness to prose; there are no rhyming lines. Shakespeare adopted this same style of writing in his own plays.

Here is an example of blank verse taken from *A Midsummer Night's Dream:*

> Hippolyta, I wooed thee with my sword And won thy
>     love doing thee injuries. But I will wed thee in
>     another key,
> With pomp, with triumph, and with reveling.[31]

Another style similarity was the development of characters and the events which take place. Readers and historians have drawn parallels between Marlowe's *Dr. Faustus* and Shakespeare's *Richard III*.

Richard III states:

> Cold fearful drops stand on my trembling flesh.
> What do I fear? Myself? There's none else by.
> Richard loves Richard; that is, I and I.[32]

Richard is aware of his isolation, in tune with his guilt and misery. *Dr. Faustus* features a similar scene, in which the main character undergoes the same type of self-realization:

> See, see where Christ's blood streams in the
>     firmament!
> One drop would save my soul – half a drop: ah, my
>     Christ!
> Ah, rend not my heart for naming of my Christ! Yet will I
>     call on him: O spare me, Lucifer—

Faustus is also keenly aware that his death is imminent. Both characters refer to death and to some sort of "drop," either sweat or blood, which could be references to Christ. Both make suppositions for their lives to be saved even though they know their afterlife fates are sure to be doomed.[33]

While both plays premiered in the same year, historians believe Marlowe was the originator of the idea while Shakespeare was influenced by him.

Historians have also compared Shakespeare's *Richard II* with Marlowe's *Edward II*; the latter debuted in 1593, *Richard II* in 1595. Both stories focus on the fall from grace of a king. Noting this, author John Bakeless made the following observation:

Shakespeare's play, like Marlowe's, has a fiery dispute near the beginning. In *Richard II*, this is between Bolingbroke and Mowbray; in *Edward the Second*, between the king and his nobles. In each play the quarrel serves to bring the opposing factions into line against each other and reveal the general nature of the plot at once. In each play there are three king's favorites: Gaveston and the two Spensers in *Edward the Second*, Busby, Green, and Bagot in *Richard II*...

Each king is caught unprepared by the return of an absent enemy. Each is forced, after a hesitation of which each author makes full dramatic use, to abdicate. Each, in his anger, destroys a physical object: Edward a letter, Richard a mirror. Each is eventually murdered, and the coffin of each is brought on the stage in the final scene.[34]

Another literary influence on Shakespeare was the Middle English poet Geoffrey Chaucer. The author was best known for his book *The Canterbury Tales*.

Shakespeare's tragedy *Troilus and Cressida* was taken from Chaucer's poem *Troilus and Criseyde*. Chaucer's "The Knight's Tale" may have prompted Shakespeare to pen *The Two Noble Kinsmen*.

Shakespeare's writings were also influenced by Plutarch. In fact, Shakespeare borrowed Plutarch's *Parallel*

*Lives* for use in creating the plays *Antony and Cleopatra, Coriolanus,* and *Julius Caesar*.[35]

The Bible played an immense role in influencing the art and literary works produced in Shakespeare's time. Religion was a hot button topic. During the reign of Elizabeth I, it was politically mandated that all her subjects must attend the Anglican church. This was known as the Act Against Recusants of 1593 and, while it was not illegal to be a Catholic, it was severely frowned upon.[36]

In 1987, scholar Naseeb Shaheen published a book outlining the biblical references in Shakespeare's plays. For instance, Katherine's final monologue in *The Taming of the Shrew* rehashes the biblical argument that women are to be faithful to their husbands. She states:

> A woman moved is like a fountain troubled,
> Muddy, ill-seeming, thick, bereft of beauty,
> And while it is so, none so dry or thirsty
> Will deign to sip or touch one drop of it.
> Thy husband is thy lord, thy life, thy keeper,
> Thy head, thy sovereign; one that cares for thee
> And for thy maintenance; commits his body
> To painful labor both by sea and land,
> To watch the night in storms, the day in cold,
> Whilst thou li'st warm at home, secure and safe;
> And craves no other tribute at thy hands
> But love, fair looks, and true obedience—

Too little payment for so great a debt.[37]

When compared to the following Bible passage, one can see the influence:

> Wives, submit yourselves unto your own husbands, as unto the Lord.
> For the husband is the head of the wife, even as Christ is the head of the church: and he is the saviour of the body.
> Therefore as the church is subject unto Christ, so let the wives be to their own husbands in everything.[38]

Ephesians 5:22-33 of the King James Bible advises women to be faithful to and maintain their duty to their husbands. Katherine asks the other female characters in the play to do the same. Both texts present the debt women must pay to their husbands as a small price in return for what is bestowed upon them by their providers.

Another idea taken straight from the Bible is Satan. Shakespeare's plots imitate that of the Bible in suggesting Satan uses Scripture to tempt people away from Christ. Corinthians 11:13-14 warns of those who put on a false face to tempt others, after learning tricks from the Devil himself:

> For such are false apostles, deceitful workers,
> transforming themselves into apostles of
> Christ. And no wonder! For Satan himself
> transforms himself into an angel of light.[39]

A similar thought is put forth by Banquo in *Macbeth*:

> But 'tis strange.
> And oftentimes, to win us to our harm,
> The instruments of darkness tell us truths,
> Win us with honest trifles, to betray's
> In deepest consequence.[40]

Other religious themes touched upon by Shakespeare include the idea of forgiveness, loving thy neighbor, resisting temptation, and the eternal combat between good and evil.

The influence on Shakespeare of Marlowe and other writers, as well as the Bible, is undeniable, and the research supporting these claims is abundant. However, there are other sources from which the great English bard drew his inspiration.

Shakespeare included the local landscape in his plays, especially that of his native England. There are many references throughout his work to the countryside and to nature; in various plays Nature even becomes a character, acting as either good or evil.

Shakespeare includes a certain reverence of nature in his characters' soliloquies. For example, in his play *The Tempest*, Caliban speaks of his island and the days in which another character, Prospero, was new to the landscape:

> When thou camest first,
> Thou strokedst me and madest much of me, wouldst
>     give me
> Water with berries in't, and teach me how
> To name the bigger light, and how the less,
> That burn by day and night: and then I loved thee
> And show'd thee all the qualities o' the isle,
> The fresh springs, brine-pits, barren place and fertile:[41]

Shakespeare and King were influenced by their own lives, by the writers that came before them, and by the landscapes that surrounded them, both the external environment and the cultural ideals they grew up with. They were both influenced by their personal beliefs and values. Both men wrote extensively about what it means to be human, about the struggle between doing the right thing and giving in to temptation.

During Shakespeare's time, characters in plays had clearly defined roles; mainly, there were the heroes, the villains, and the fools. Shakespeare was one of the first writers to portray the element of suffering in a villain, thereby attributing to the bad guy those natural human qualities we all share. Sympathy for the villain had been nonexistent until Shakespeare struck an empathetic cord with his audiences.

King explores the complex nature of the human condition equally well in his novels. Jack Torrance wants to provide for his family, yet he too weak to fight off the evil that surrounds him. He eventually goes on a bloody rampage against his wife and child. In the midst of it, however, he feels love for his son and encourages him to escape.

Jack is therefore not the kind of one-dimensional villain audiences are used to. Neither is Carrie. Although she had been bullied and abused, her choice to kill everyone at the high school dance is, obviously, extreme. But this kind of revenge allows for deep insight into the deepest reaches of our shared humanity.

Hamlet is a perfect example of this: he is cast into despair, muses over the deaths of others, kills his uncle, and is eventually killed himself. The varied qualities Shakespeare gave each of his characters was unprecedented at the time. King has continued the tradition.

# CHAPTER 4.
# WHERE DID THEY GET THEIR INSPIRATION?

Many of the characters that grace Shakespeare's plays are memorable. One of his most loveable characters appears repeatedly: the fool.

An oaf who fumbles and stumbles, puts his foot in his mouth, and sometimes does more harm than good, the fool speaks his mind with the purest of intentions. For centuries the fool has appeared in literature. He or she makes an appearance in novels and plays, as well as in television shows and films, providing comic relief within the plot.

Shakespeare's iconic fools, however, were said to be inspired by the English playwright Robert Armin. Also an actor, Armin landed many of the leading roles in Shakespeare's plays. He got his start in acting after befriending a famous English clown. Richard Tarlton saw in Armin a stroke of comedic ingenuity and took the young man under his wing.

Armin played the role of Dogberry in Shakespeare's *Much Ado About Nothing*, as well as Touchstone in *As You Like It*. There is some evidence to indicate the role of Touchstone was created exclusively for Armin. The character is insightful, witty, and able to expose the true nature of the people that surround him, so he is indeed a touchstone. The role was Armin's first comic part in a Shakespeare play.[42]

After the two men began to work together, Shakespeare might have based other jester type characters on Armin. The Fool in *King Lear*, for example.

Armin had previously published works in which he explored the fool or jester character; he stated that the jester is a darker character who is "kept" in the court by a King.

In *King Lear*, the Fool is exactly that, a comedian whose sole purpose is to provide comic relief for the King. Yet Shakespeare's Fool is the only character that has the freedom to criticize King Lear. Instead of punishing the Fool, the king accepts his jabs.

In *As You Like It*, the fool character is honest and extremely intelligent. He provides advice as well as criticism. These were qualities Armin possessed. So perhaps the character in the play was based on him.

Armin also played the role of Feste in *Twelfth Night*. The character was known as a "licensed fool," the sole clown for Olivia. Like the Fool in *King Lear*, he was free to say whatever he pleased. There is a whimsical air to Feste that suits the lightheartedness of the Twelfth Night festivities. He makes use of witty repartee and quick quips to communicate. He is also known for his astute ability to surmise a situation, gather details about the other characters, and anticipate events that will soon take place.

It is quite mysterious that Shakespeare never credited Armin in any of the sources for his work.

Shakespeare did give credit to the poet Arthur Brooke. Brooke was inspired by the Italian poet Bandello, who took inspiration from a French poet. The work that was passed down through these writers would eventually be published in 1562 in the form of Brooke's *The Tragicall Historye of Romeus and Juliet*.

Unlike in Shakespeare's version of the same story, Brooke does not make clear the struggle between the two families.

### The Argument
Love hath inflaméd twain by sudden sight,
And both do grant the thing that both desire
They wed in shrift by counsel of a friar.

Young Romeus climbs fair Juliet's bower by night.

Three months he doth enjoy his chief delight.

By Tybalt's rage provokéd unto ire,

He payeth death to Tybalt for his hire.

A banished man he 'scapes by secret flight.

New marriage is offered to his wife.

She drinks a drink that seems to reave her breath:

They bury her that sleeping yet hath life.

Her husband hears the tidings of her death.

He drinks his bane. And she with Romeus' knife,

When she awakes, herself, alas! she slay'th.[43]

Brooke's opening segment differs from Shakespeare's Prologue:

Two households, both alike in dignity,

In fair Verona, where we lay our scene,

From ancient grudge break to new mutiny,

Where civil blood makes civil hands unclean.

From forth the fatal loins of these two foes

A pair of star-cross'd lovers take their life;

Whose misadventured piteous overthrows

Do with their death bury their parents' strife.

The fearful passage of their death-mark'd love,

And the continuance of their parents' rage,

Which, but their children's end, nought could remove,

Is now the two hours' traffic of our stage;

The which if you with patient ears attend,
What here shall miss, our toil shall strive to mend.[44]

Both sections do include the fate of the two lovers. Yet it was Shakespeare that offered a moral to the story.

One real life event which is said to have shaped Shakespeare's work was the death of his son in 1596. His son was named Hamnet.

In writing the play *Hamlet*, Shakespeare deftly incorporated his own grief. Though the details of his son's death are not confirmed, it is believed Shakespeare was away in London working when his eleven-year-old son fell ill. News spread slowly in those days. By the time the father heard that he needed to come home immediately, the illness was worse.

It is believed that by the time Shakespeare reached Stratford-upon-Avon, Hamnet had already passed away. The burial records are confirmed by the Holy Trinity Church.

Although the play Hamlet, Prince of Denmark, had already been written and performed in England, Shakespeare created his own version. And at the time, the name Hamnet was interchangeable with Hamlet in regard to spelling and pronunciation.[45]

The effect of his son's sudden death can also be observed in *King John*, a play about the life of the former King of England, the son of Henry II.

In this play, Constance wants her son Arthur to ascend to the throne of England. She finds out he has been captured. After she is accused of being mad, she defends herself:

> Young Arthur is my son, and he is lost:
> I am not mad: I would to heaven I were!
> For then, 'tis like I should forget myself:
> O, if I could, what grief should I forget!
> Preach some philosophy to make me mad,
> And thou shalt be canonized, cardinal;
> For being not mad but sensible of grief,
> My reasonable part produces reason
> How I may be deliver'd of these woes,
> And teaches me to kill or hang myself.

Shakespeare is also well known for his sonnets. In writing these rhyming poems, he was influenced by the Italian poet Petrarch. Although there are subtle differences between Petrarchian and Shakespearean sonnets, the content is similar.

For example, Petrarch emptied his soul when writing about Laura, his true love. The sonnets about her are musical in form, conveying a deep passion. However, the lines are so complex in phrasing that the poems are difficult to understand.

Shakespeare adopted the same kind of figurativeness in his sonnets, utilizing complex descriptions. The abstract language requires more than a few close readings to decipher meaning.

Shakespeare's sonnets were published in 1609 and featured a dedication to a mysterious "W.H." Some think the initials belong to a woman, but not Shakespeare's wife. Others believe the "W.H." is a reference to Shakespeare himself and the "H" was supposed to be an "S." A third hypotheses posits the "W.H." as being a reference to a male friend of Shakespeare's.

Whatever the subject or inspiration for the sonnets, the figure of the woman in these works is a captivating character. She possesses great charm, and is perhaps a fusion of the best characteristics of all the men and women with whom Shakespeare was acquainted.[46]

## King's Inspirations

Like Shakespeare once did, Stephen King draws his inspiration from real life people and events. However, King does not borrow his characters, titles, and plots from other writers. Times have changed and a modern day writer would get sued for doing so.

King has admitted that he gets his ideas and inspiration from "seeing two things and having them come together in some new and interesting way, and then adding the question, 'What if ?'"[47]

For example, the inspiration for writing the novel *Carrie* was two real girls King knew in high school. Both were shy, reserved, and picked-on. In King's version of the school victim, Carrie discovers her hidden powers and develops the psychic agency to be used against her tormentors.

King has stated that he envisioned the shower scene before anything else, drawing inspiration from the janitorial position he maintained one summer at Brunswick High in Maine. When he cleaned the girls' bathroom, he noticed the pink shower curtains. The boys' shower room had no curtains. In his mind, King immediately crafted the shower scene that is so central to the plot.[48]

Years before, however, King had read an article about telekinesis and people who claimed to have special powers. In writing the novel *Carrie*, he fused together the two ideas – the girls' locker room and telekinesis. Since the characters are based on real people, this makes them come to life on paper and, eventually, on the big screen.

In 1976, King's novel *Rage* was released under the pen name Richard Bachman. *Rage* tells the story of high school student Charlie Decker who has just been expelled for hitting his chemistry teacher with a wrench. Charlie goes to his locker, takes out a pistol, and lights his locker on fire. Then he goes in a classroom and shoots his algebra teacher.

When the students in the room try to escape, Charlie orders them to remain in the classroom. He holds the students hostage for four hours while he plays mind games with members of the faculty who try to talk him out of the situation.

Charlie admits to the other students that he was abused by his father. He then encourages them to tell to their secrets as well. The police finally enter the building and make a failed attempt to kill Charlie. He is later sent to a psychiatric hospital.

King drew inspiration for the story from his own high school experience, which he has described as frustrating. King said he wrote the first draft of the story when he was in high school. This would have been viewed as an indication of troubled mental health if anyone had read the story at the time.[49]

The next book he published was *The Shining*. The plot for this novel was inspired by two related events, a hotel stay and a dream.

In the fall of 1974, Stephen and his wife Tabitha had stayed at the Stanley Hotel in Estes Park, Colorado. The hotel is massive, historic, and breathtaking with the majestic Rocky Mountains as backdrop. The night King and his wife stayed there, however, they were the only guests. This was because as the staff was preparing to close down the hotel for the coming winter months.

As King walked the empty halls, he imagined ghosts running through the building. When he went to bed that night, he had a dream that his son was being pursued by a fire hose. When King awoke, he was left with the outline of the story which would eventually become *The Shining*.

King brings to life the father figure of Jack Torrance. Clearly influenced by his own father, King creates a loving and murderous character who can trick his son into trusting him.

In a frightful scene, Jack pursues his son Danny, mallet in hand. Danny hears the voice of his father summoning him in the way only a father would:

"Danny? You can come out, doc. Just a little spanking, that's all. Take it like a man and it will be all over. We don't need her, doc. Just you and me, right? When we get this little...spanking... behind us, it will be just you and me."

In an act of genuine love and concern, Jack has a moment of clarity – a pause in the possession at the hands of the evil spirits in the hotel. He coaches his son to "Run away. Quick. And remember how much I love you."

This statement perfectly depicts the conflict that exists between Jack and Danny, and between King and his own father.

Securing the job at the hotel might have brought the family financial stability, at least for the winter. And it was also Jack's job to protect wife and son from the evil that plagued the Overlook. Jack failed on both accounts.

Nevertheless, Danny still attempts to rescue his father. Jack fails his son and is killed.

The presence of the author in the story is two-fold: one, as an adoring father who dreamed of his son being chased. This King is depicted in the Jack who encourages his son to run away and remember his love for him. The other King, however, is Danny, not protected by an untrustworthy father.

As is classic in King's novels, childhood innocence is exalted when as Danny survives the hotel spirits and the explosion in the hotel basement.

In 1986, King published *It* which tells the story of seven different children who are haunted by the It of the title. It takes the form of a clown when it terrorizes the characters.

King has said the inspiration for the book came to him in the late 1970s while he was living in Boulder, Colorado. The family was on their way home from eating lunch at a pizzeria when the transmission fell off the car. They were stranded on the side of the road.

A few days later, the mechanic called to say that King could pick up the car whenever he wished. He decided to walk the three miles to the auto body shop. On this walk, he became aware of how scary his footsteps on a wooden bridge sounded, and how eerie the twilight was as it played around him. He felt like there was some type of creature living under the bridge. He felt vulnerable.

He was further inspired by the fairytale "The Three Billy-Goats Gruff." The story tells about three goats that must cross a bridge owned by a troll. King decided to write a story in which children would have to get past their tormentor in the same way. This became "It."

Instead of under a bridge, however, the shape-shifting evil entity lived under the streets in the sewer.[51]

Momentary images and fleeting thoughts had time and again proven to be meaty writing prompts for King throughout his career. The plot for *Christine*, for instance, came to him while he was driving his car. As he watched the odometer roll over from 9,999.9 to 10,000 miles, he was struck with an immediate image. What if a car could control the odometer and make it go backwards? *Christine* evolved as the author developed the characters and their relationships.[52]

A similar scenario played out one day when King was at the beach. He noticed a young boy in a wheelchair flying a kite. The snapshot that he took in his mind laid the groundwork for the story that would eventually become *Joyland*, a novel published in 2013. The story chronicles the murder of a young girl, the ghosts that possess the haunted house where she was killed, and boys who attempt to solve the mystery.

King has admitted that his writing process is no longer the same as it once was. Through the years, he has undergone some changes – some intentional, some unintentional.

In 2012, King spoke about his writing process to a group of students at the University of Massachusetts

Lowell. He told them that he used to plot out his stories and take notes, but he had abandoned that practice to write about topics on a whim. He said the inspiration for a book can come from something as simple as a news broadcast. Then he referenced a story on television that had recently sparked something in his mind.

The news report focused on a woman who had discovered her husband was cheating on her. She tracked down the other woman and, in an attempt to harm her, accidentally backed a car over innocent people instead. King told the students he had decided to write a story based on those events, making minor changes to the details.

What started as a news report would become King's 2014 novel *Mr. Mercedes.* The story is about a man who drives his car into a crowd of people at a job fair.

Everyday life served as the most important influence on the works of these two famous authors. Although social and cultural norms were vastly different for William Shakespeare and Stephen King, they displayed the same keen interest in human emotion and behavior. Both men were influenced by the people and events in their own lives.

# CHAPTER 5.
# TURNING POINTS IN THEIR CAREERS

Because very little is known about Shakespeare's life from around 1585 to 1592, historians can only speculate he spent these seven years caring for his family, traveling around seeking resources for his plays, and perhaps working as an actor or as a teacher. He must have also been honing his skills as a playwright. Some historians claim he was gaining steady prominence as an actor in and around London, so he was most likely recruited to be part of an acting troupe.

In 1592, the first recorded information on Shakespeare since his marriage to Anne Hathaway was documented. The reference appeared in the autobiography of Robert Greene, a dramatist. He evidently did not take a liking to Shakespeare:

> "There is an upstart crow, beautified with our
> feathers, that with his Tygers heart wrapt in a
> Players hide supposes he is as well able to bombast
> out a blank verse as the best of you; and, being
> an absolute Johannes Factotum, is in his own
> conceit the only Shake-scene in a country."[53]

The scathing review may be due to the fact that Shakespeare was new to the playwriting scene at the time, still an unknown. Greene was already well known and did not approve of the newcomer.

Shakespeare was beginning to draw attention to himself and his art. The portrait painted of Shakespeare in the book was so offensive, however, that Greene's editor, Henry Chettle, felt the need to apologize to the bard. Apparently, Greene had been on his deathbed and had managed to offend not just Shakespeare but a few others.

Chettle wrote:

> "The other, whom at that time I did not so much
> spare as since I wish I had, for that, as I have
> moderated the heat of living writers and might have
> used my own discretion (especially in such a case,
> the author being dead), that I did not I am as sorry
> as if the original fault had been my fault, because
> myself have seen his demeanor no less civil than

he excellent in the quality he professes. Besides, the diver of worship have reported his uprightness of dealing, which argues his honesty, and his facetious grace in writing that approves his art."[54]

Chettle's published apology indicates that Shakespeare was held in high-esteem, so the editor did not want to offend him. The plays *Titus Andronicus* and *Henry VI* were already well-known productions, motivating Chettle to apologize on behalf of his deceased client.

Historians point to the year 1593 as a pivotal year in Shakespeare's career. The plague had been sweeping through England and the spread of the disease was rampant. This is because London was overpopulated, infested with rats, fleas, and other vermin that carried the disease-causing bacteria. In those days, people had no idea how to prevent the spread of disease. They did not understand that the illness was passed person to person and via the sewage waste that polluted the streets and the waters.

Understandably, during the plague people were not attending the theater. So historians believe Shakespeare took this time to stay inside, writing. He managed to avoid contracting the plague. Many theaters and playhouses ended up closing for the duration of the disease outbreak.

During this time, Henry Wriothesley, the third Earl of Southampton, took note of the bard's work. The Earl became one of Shakespeare's patrons.

Because of this newfound support, Shakespeare was able to publish his poem *Venus and Adonis*. The publication established his reputation as a great poet and illustrated his deft skill with writing sexual content.

*Venus and Adonis* is said to be one of Shakespeare's most sexual works. The poem describes the fleeting relationships between the Adonis, a hunter, and Venus, the love goddess.

Although Venus at first attempts to avoid Adonis, she later succumbs to his advances. Shakespeare dedicated this work entirely to the Earl of Southampton, stating in the inscription:

> I KNOW not how I shall offend in dedicating my unpolished lines to your lordship, nor how the world will censure me for choosing so strong a prop to support so weak a burden only, if your honour seem but pleased, I account myself highly praised, and vow to take advantage of all idle hours, till I have honoured you with some graver labour. But if the first heir of my invention prove deformed, I shall be sorry it had so noble a god-father, and never after ear so barren a

land, for fear it yield me still so bad a harvest. I leave it to your honourable survey, and your honour to your heart's content; which I wish may always answer your own wish and the world's hopeful expectation.[55]

The next year, Shakespeare wrote *The Rape of Lucrece* and it was published in May of 1594. The poem was again dedicated to the Earl of Southampton. This one chronicled the rape of Lucrece by Tarquin. Overcome with shame and grief, Lucrece commits suicide.

That same year, the theaters reopened and Shakespeare was able to return to his plays. His popularity increased after he became a member of Lord Chamberlain's Men, a theater company. It was there that he was introduced to the actor Richard Burbage, who would go on to star in many of Shakespeare's works including *Hamlet*. It was also during this time that Shakespeare acted in some of the minor roles in his own plays, establishing himself as a skilled actor.

As an actor traveling with Lord Chamberlain's Men, Shakespeare performed for Elizabeth I multiple times, a great honor. He received ten pounds for each of his performances.

While he was not acting for Lord Chamberlain's Men, he was diligently crafting his plays. During this time he wrote *Richard II, Romeo & Juliet, Love's Labour's Lost*, and *King John*.

The sudden passage of eleven year old Hamnet in 1596 was a turning point for Shakespeare. He did not spend much time with his family when he was working for the theater troupe, and this may have caused him guilt. When he returned home for his son's funeral, historians claim he took up a new interest in his hometown. With the money he had saved from acting and publishing his works, he purchased a house. Known as New Place, the home was the second largest house in town.

Although the New Place is gone now, the Shakespeare Birthplace Trust purchased the land for historical purposes. It was in this house that Shakespeare took his last breath in 1616.[56]

Wihile he was still touring with Lord Chamberlain's Men, the company had a lease with the Blackfriars Theatre. In 1597, the lease agreement ended, leaving the troupe virtually homeless. This meant they needed a location to perform their plays.

At this point, the troupe was comprised of Burbage and Shakespeare, along with James Burbage, G. Byran, Augustine Phillips, John Hemminges, Will Sly, and Thomas Pope. They decided to build a new theater house.

However, they lacked the necessary funds to begin a project of this magnitude.

The Burbage brothers were able to come up with half of the necessary funds. So it was the responsibility of the remaining members to come up with the other half. Everyone found the means to contribute and they kicked off the construction of the theater. Thus, Shakespeare owned 12.5 percent of what would become the Globe Theater.

Construction began in 1599. Only months later, the theater opened their first production, Shakespeare's play *Julius Caesar*.

Written above the main entryway to the theater is the message in Latin *"Totus mundus agit histrionem."* This translates to "the whole world is a playhouse." Or as Shakespeare states in *As You Like It*, "All the world's a stage."[57]

## King's Turning Points

Fortunately for historians and fans, Stephen King outlined the major turning points in his life in his book *On Writing: A Memoir of the Craft*. He provided key insights into his writing process, the thoughts that run through his mind when he is crafting plots and characters, and the hardships he faced as a young writer.

Before the debut publication of *Carrie*, King had written a handful of novels. Of these, he recalls:

> "Two of them were bad, one was indifferent, and I thought two of them were pretty good. The two good ones were *Getting It On* (which became *Rage* when it was finally published) and *The Long Walk*...
>
> I submitted *Walk* to the Bennett Cerf/Random House first-novel competition in the fall of 1967 and it was promptly rejected with a form note...no comment of any kind. Hurt and depressed, sure that the book must really be terrible, I stuck it into the fabled TRUNK, which all novelists, both published and aspiring, carry around. I never submitted it again until Elaine Geiger at New American Library asked if [Richard Bachman] was going to follow up *Rage*."[58]

King completed a novel, *The Long Walk*, while he was still in college. He was so excited about it that he submitted it to his professor for review.

Professor Burt Hatlen was impressed that King "was somebody who really knew how to tell a story, that grabbed you and kept you going ... I don't know that that's something that can be taught, and he clearly had it." The novel was not published until 1979. It was released under King's pseudonym Richard Bachman. Despite early rejections, *The Long Walk* was rated by the American Library Association as one of the top one hundred best books for teens.[59]

The second major turning point in his career was his novel *Carrie*. Up until that point, King was accustomed to a life of economic limitation. He had not grown up with money. He married young and the couple had their first child in the early 1970s. He took odd jobs in addition to his work as an English teacher. They lived in a trailer.

King was crafting his stories on his wife's typewriter. He sent them to magazines that paid well, like *Penthouse* and *Playboy*.

Not long after the birth of their second child, King got an offer from the school where he was teaching to work as an advisor for the Debate Club. The position paid three hundred dollars a year. King wanted to take the job, but his wife told him not to. Tabitha said it would leave no time for his writing.

Shortly after that, he sat down at his wife's typewriter with a fresh idea about a high school loner tormented by her peers. The storyline began to play out in his mind and he found himself wondering, "What if the girl that nobody likes wanted revenge and had the power to kill with her mind?"[60]

King started typing and, before he knew it, he had a few pages. But when he reread them, he was disgusted. So he crumpled them up and threw them in the trash.

In one of King's biographies, what is said to have happened in the days following that moment are crucial:

> "The next evening, when King came home from work, his wife ... had the pages in hand. She'd taken the crumpled, ash-smeared pages from the garbage. 'She wanted to know the rest of the story,' King remembered. 'I told her I didn't know ... about high school girls. She said she'd help me with that part ... 'You've got something here,' she said. 'I really think you do.'

Inspired by her encouragement, King finished the manuscript and submitted it for publication. *Carrie* was rejected by dozens of publishing companies.[61]

So King figured this would be the fourth novel he would stash away in some drawer or trunk. *Carrie* would surely meet the same fate as the novels that came before it: *Rage*, *The Long Walk*, and *Blaze*, all still unpublished.

Prepping himself for more rejection, King sent the manuscript to Doubleday Publishing in January of

1973. Two months later, he received incredible news: Doubleday liked his manuscript and was offering him $2,500 in advance to purchase the rights.

After this amazing news, King's luck shifted. An offer was made for the paperback rights to the book in the astounding amount of $400,000. Once the deal was worked out, half the money would be King's.[62]

Considering the international popularity King now enjoys, it is hard to imagine his life of struggle. In reflecting on the number of times he was rejected and the fortitude he maintained to keep writing, King writes:

> "I have spent a good many years since—too many, I think—being ashamed about what I write. I think I was forty before I realized that almost every writer of fiction or poetry who has ever published a line has been accused by someone of wasting his or her God-given talent. If you write (or paint or dance or sculpt or sing, I suppose), someone will try to make you feel lousy about it, that's all."[63]

The final turning point in King's career was the publication of his book *It* in 1986. Although King was, at that point, a household name and a successful author, the novel represented a shift in his storytelling technique. The new literary style in *It* signaled a departure from his earlier novels. He used multiple points of view. *It* moves fast, with scenes changing rapidly, as opposed to the longer, more detailed style used in his earlier works.

*It* was lauded as the best-selling book of the year, grossing him immense profits from the sale of the book and from the television and film adaptations that followed. There were discussion about additional film adaptations spearheaded by the big production companies including Warner Bros.[64]

Both Shakespeare and King faced early struggles and challenging difficulties on the path to immense success. Both men were forced to deal with personal hardships and economic challenges before achieving fame and the associated rewards.

But what would have happened if the plague had not spread wildly and shut down the city of London, forcing Shakespeare inside, where he dedicated his time and energy to his writing? What if Tabitha King had not found in the wastebasket the crumpled pages of what would become her husband's first successful novel, *Carrie?*

# CHAPTER 6.
# NEWSWORTHY MOMENTS AND CONTROVERSY

Doubt has plagued Shakespeare's biographers for centuries. They have been forced to deal with faulty records, misspellings, missing years on record, and lost documents.

One of the well-established records in Shakespeare's life was the marriage to Anne Hathaway. However, other records have emerged to complicate the story of his marriage. There are, in fact, two documents: a record of a marriage to Anne Whateley; and a record of the marriage to Anne Hathaway. Both records were documented in late November 1582.

This has given rise to three theories regarding Shakespeare's marriage. The first is that the marriage clerk accidentally wrote Whateley instead of Hathaway on the record of the marriage between Anne Whateley and WM Shaxpere recorded in Temple Grafton. The second theory is that there was, coincidentally, one couple named Anne Whateley and WM Shaxpere who married in Temple Grafton and another couple named WM Shagspere and Anne Hathwey who were married in Shakespeare's home town of Stratford.

The third theory is that there were, in fact, two Annes: one Shakespeare was in love with, and another whom Shakespeare felt obliged to marry.

Anne Hathaway was three months pregnant with Shakespeare's child, hence the obligation he felt to marry her. But, the theory goes, he was actually in love with Anne Whateley.

In fact, Shakespeare legally married Anne Hathaway. The couple had their first child, Susanna, in 1583, followed by twins Judith and Hamnet in January of 1585. Anne disappeared from historical records after the birth of her twins except for a recording after the death of Hamnet.[65]

As with his birth and marriage, there is mystery surrounding the bard's death. One night, apparently after a round of heavy drinking with friends, Shakespeare contracted a fatal fever. There is not much evidence to suggest the actual cause of death was alcohol consumption. In fact, at the time there was an outbreak of typhus which is known to produce fever-like symptoms.

In a biography written about Shakespeare's son-in-law, who was also his doctor, author C. Martin Mitchell states that the cause of death might have been "in the nature of a cerebral hemorrhage or apoplexy that quickly deepened and soon became fatal."[66]

Mitchell claims that the stress inherent in Shakespeare's career ultimately killed him. At the time of the poet's death, however, there were many diseases in London that could have afflicted the bard. In addition to typhus, city residents died from smallpox, syphilis, tuberculosis, malaria, and a host of other lethal ills.

A further romanticizing of Shakespeare's life states that he died on his birthday. In the will he drafted in 1611, he left his "second best bed" to his wife. He willed all of his property to his eldest daughter Susanna, and three hundred pounds to his other daughter Judith. This too is mysterious.

There are also speculations and rumors regarding the bard's sexuality. Research seems to indicate that Shakespeare was romantically involved with another man. This might have been his patron Henry Wriothesley, possibly someone else.

In Sonnet 20, part of the 154 sonnets Shakespeare wrote during his lifetime, he states:

A woman's face with Nature's own hand painted
Hast thou, the master-mistress of my passion;
A woman's gentle heart, but not acquainted
With shifting change, as is false women's fashion;
An eye more bright than theirs, less false in rolling,
Gilding the object whereupon it gazeth;
A man in hue, all hues in his controlling,
Much steals men's eyes and women's souls amazeth.
And for a woman wert thou first created;
Till Nature, as she wrought thee, fell a-doting,
And by addition me of thee defeated,
By adding one thing to my purpose nothing.
But since she prick'd thee out for women's pleasure,
Mine be thy love and thy love's use their treasure.[67]

Here, Shakespeare describes his feelings toward men, stating they are just as beautiful as women yet have no need to wear makeup. And in the last couple of lines he seems to be encouraging men to save their love for him.

Another source used to back up the claim that Shakespeare had a male lover is Sonnet 126:

O thou, my lovely boy, who in thy power
Dost hold Time's fickle glass, his sickle, hour;
Who hast by waning grown, and therein show'st
Thy lovers withering as thy sweet self grow'st;
If Nature, sovereign mistress over wrack,

As thou goest onwards, still will pluck thee back,
She keeps thee to this purpose, that her skill
May time disgrace and wretched minutes kill.
Yet fear her, O thou minion of her pleasure;
She may detain, but not still keep, her treasure:
Her audit, though delay'd, answer'd must be,
And her quietus is to render thee.[68]

This sonnet reads like an ode to a young boy, lamenting that even *he* is inescapable from the effects of Nature and the passage of Time. No one knows for sure who "my lovely boy" refers to. It might be himself, his son, or just boys in general.

Shakespeare's plays were performed by all-male casts. That was the tradition during the time, and Shakespeare had no choice but to select male actors for all of his roles. However, there is speculation that the word "drag" originated from Shakespeare's stage direction. The term refers to dressing as a woman, and it may have come from the fact that Shakespeare noted "Dressed as girls" to signify the parts in which men would play the female roles.[69]

If the rumors about Shakespeare's homosexual relations are true, the poet would have broken English law. An English law passed during the reign of King Henry

VIII stated quite clearly that anyone who engaged in a homosexual act could be put to death.[70]

Since it was commonplace during the time for men to have close relationships with one another, any controversial content in Shakespeare's sonnets and plays would have gone unnoticed. The fact that he dedicated much of his work to his patron was unremarkable since he was indeed grateful to the man who had financially supported him.

## Controversy and Stephen King

Stephen King met his future wife when they were college students at the University of Maine. The two attended the same writing seminar. Tabitha was familiar with his writing as she had read his work in the school newspaper. King's weekly column was called "The Garbage Truck."

In his memoir, King said:

> "We met when we were working in a library, and I fell in love with her during a poetry workshop in the fall of 1969, when I was a senior and Tabby was a junior. I fell in love with her partly because I understood what she was doing with her work. I fell in love with her because *she* understood what she was doing with it."[71]

They were married on January 7, 1971, shortly after the birth of their daughter Naomi. The couple would go on to have sons Joseph in 1972, and Owen in 1977.

Tabitha dedicated more than a decade to helping her husband with his novels. She eventually returned to writing herself, and in 1981 she published a novel. *Small World* tells the story of the daughter of a former President, the journalist who tries to uncover dirty information about her, and the man who changes the life of the journalist.[72]

King frequently took the children on long car trips. In order to pass the time, he played audio books in the car. The books he liked were not always available on tape, so he had his children read aloud the stories he wanted to hear. He had his children reading everything from *Anna Karenina* to the works of horror writer Dean Koontz.

In 2013, the *New York Times* profiled the adult King children:

> "Entertaining their parents, for the King children, was part job, part enrichment. At bedtime, they were the ones expected to tell their parents stories, instead of the other way around. Whatever their methods or intentions, Stephen and Tabitha's shared vocation, and their approach to child rearing, has yielded a

significant number of successful fiction writers in their household. Tabitha is an accomplished writer with eight novels to her credit, and two of their three children, Joe and Owen, are novelists."[73]

Stephen King experienced troubling times in the late 1980s. While in his office one night, he suddenly collapsed on the floor. He was unconscious for some time before regaining his faculties. When he woke up, he was covered in blood.

During this time in his life, King had been abusing drugs and alcohol, namely beer and cocaine, frequently at the same time. The beer had knocked him out, the coke had made his nose bleed.

King had started drinking beer at the age of eighteen, but he had not been troubled by it. However, as he got older, he came to rely on the alcohol, then drugs, for stress relief.

He has stated that this period of his life is a blur. In fact, he does not remember the books he wrote throughout most of the decade.

After he passed out, however, his wife stepped in. King described what happened:

"Tabby began by dumping a trash bag full of stuff from my office out on the rug: beer cans, cigarette butts, cocaine in gram bottles and cocaine in plastic Baggies, coke spoons caked with snot and blood, Valium, Xanax, bottles of Robitussin cough syrup and NyQuil cold medicine, even bottles of mouthwash."[74]

He worked hard to get beyond his substance abuse and the affiliated depression. With the love and support of his family, King was able to get clean.

Then, in 1999, a series of bizarre events occurred in King's life which would have been a perfect plot for one of his horror stories.

While was taking a walk one evening near his home in Maine, he was run down by a minivan. The driver lost control of the Dodge Caravan and struck the writer from behind. King hit the windshield of the van and was thrown more than a dozen feet.

He sustained serious injuries. He had a punctured lung, one broken leg, four broken ribs, a chipped spine, and a broken hip. Thankfully, he did not have a head injury.

After undergoing surgery at Central Maine Hospital, he was determined to be in stable condition. After this, however, he had to undergo extensive physical therapy. He could only manage to take a few steps at a time when he was released from the hospital three weeks after the accident.[75]

King later purchased the van so that it would not fall into the hands of anyone looking for a hot souvenir.

Charges were not filed against the driver, who had a history of accidents and disability. A year later, the man's brother found him dead in his bed. Empty bottles of painkillers were strewn about the man's trailer home.[76]

During his lengthy recovery, King wasted no time stewing about his fate. At the hospital, he had worried about how all his notes and private papers were in his home office; anyone could have taken them while he was not around. This became the inspiration for what would become his next novel.

*Lisey's Story* is about a young woman who goes through her deceased husband's papers, eager to discover the successful novelist's unpublished work. Then a strange man begins to stalk Lisey. The man threatens her, demanding she give up the manuscript. The plot came directly from the fear King harbored in the hospital.[77]

Though the Kings have had to face challenging struggles throughout their marriage, they have been able to support one another and make it work. Together, they launched the Stephen and Tabitha King Foundation to help serve the people of Maine. The charity helps fund authors and libraries. For instance, in 2013, they committed to paying $3 million toward a total $9 million renovation of a historic library in Bangor.[78]

Their own life stories played a significant role in the careers of both William Shakespeare and Stephen King. While the events, issues, and controversies made for good stories, they also provided inspiration for the authors' work.

While the world may never know the truth about Shakespeare's life, readers have long enjoyed the man's personality, his humor, and his talent as conveyed through his writing. King's life story is available in his memoir and in the many interviews and speeches he has given over the years.

# CHAPTER 7.
# THE LATE AND THE GREAT

Near the end of his career, Shakespeare published what is now known as his collection of late romances. These plays were written in the early 1600s, right before his death.

Historians speculate that *The Tempest* was the last work Shakespeare crafted by himself. The other late romances include *Cymbeline*, *The Winter's Tale*, and *Pericles, Prince of Tyre*.

These works are whimsical, and they include mythical elements. A departure from Shakespeare's earlier works, the plays have happy-ending plotlines which feature redemption for the main characters.

*The Tempest* is the story of Prospero, a duke, and his daughter Miranda. They have been stranded on an island, sent there by Prospero's brother Antonio. On hearing that Antonio will pass by the island on a ship, Prospero conjures up a wicked storm, a tempest. The storm separates Antonio from his the rest of the men on the ship.

The men are eventually reunited and brought before Prospero. He forgives his brother, arranges a wedding for his daughter, and is free to leave the island. All of the elements that classify Shakespeare's late romances are present in *The Tempest*.

Shakespeare is said to have formally retired in 1610, and he moved out of London. He returned to Stratford-upon-Avon to the New Place, where he lived out the rest of his years with his wife and daughters.

Shakespeare's last will and testament was dated nearly one month before he passed away. This was unusual because at that time it was customary not to sign such documents until one was on one's deathbed.

Some historians speculate that Shakespeare was aware he was sick and knew he would not survive to the end of the year. He was buried in the Holy Trinity Church on April 25, 1616, two days after his death.[79]

In 1623, two of Shakespeare's colleagues compiled thirty-six of the author's plays in what would be known as *The First Folio*. The first book of its kind, the encyclopedia included the best of the playwright's work.

The preface to the folio by John Heminge and Henry Condell includes the following:

"It had bene a thing, we confesse, worthie to haue bene wished, that the Author himselfe had liu'd to haue set forth, and ouerseen his owne writings; But since it hath bin ordain'd otherwise, and he by death departed from that right, we pray you do not envie his Friends, the office of their care, and paine, to haue collected &publish'd them; and so to haue publish'd them, as where (before) you were abus'd with diuerse stolne, and surreptitious copies, maimed, and deformed by the frauds and stealthes of iniurious imposters, that expos'd them: euen those, are now offer'd to your view cur'd, and perfect of their limbes; and all the rest, absolute in their numbers, as he conceiued them."[80]

Originally titled *Mr. William Shakespeares Comedies, Histories, & Tragedies*, the collection includes the comedies *Much Ado About Nothing*, *A Midsummer Night's Dream*, and *The Taming of the Shrew*. As part of the histories section, the authors included *King John*, *Richard III*, as well as the many plays about the various King Henrys. Finally, the tragedies feature *Titus Andronicus*, *Romeo and Juliet*, *Hamlet*, and *Macbeth*.

In the years following his death, a wave of literary criticism emerged discussing Shakespeare's works. In 1668, John Dryden published an essay entitled "Of Dramatick

Poesie" in which he criticizes Shakespeare's plays on a number of topics.

The first was that Shakespeare was unable to incite in his audience any sense of passion; on the contrary, the critic states, the emotions the playwright elicited were "Lust, Cruelty, Revenge, Ambition, and those bloody actions they produc'd."[81]

Dryden found Shakespeare incapable of displaying gentleness, instead preferring to fill his plays with horror. And it was not just the negative emotions, according to Dryden, that were troubling:

> "Shakespeare lacked decorum, in Dryden's view, largely because he had written for an ignorant age and poorly educated audiences. Shakespeare excelled in 'fancy' or imagination, but he lagged behind in 'judgment.' He was a native genius, untaught, whose plays needed to be extensively rewritten to clear them of the impurities of their frequently vulgar style."[82]

Dryden was disturbed by the fact that Shakespeare wrote specifically to reach the majority of people. In defense of Shakespeare, this is what makes him so unique.

Unlike his contemporaries, Shakespeare wrote to be understood and enjoyed by the population at large. He did not write above the heads of his patrons and his audiences. Instead, he gave them what they liked.

Other criticisms emerged. According to the Aristotelian rules for drama, there should be three unities present in plays: unity of action, place, and time. This meant that plots could not have multiple timelines or too many storylines at once. Simplicity of time and action were praised.

Shakespeare notoriously broke this rule of drama. In fact, he pioneered the "tragi-comedy" in which elements of both tragedy and comedy appeared. His plots were complicated and twisting.

Samuel Johnson defended Shakespeare. The well-known literary critic wrote that there is really no need to remain faithful to the unities. The audience is well aware the stage is not real life. Time, Johnson argued, could be fluid because people understood how reality was suspended in staged productions.[83]

Perhaps one of the more bitter criticisms of Shakespeare was lodged by the influential dramatist George Bernard Shaw. Shaw stated, "There is no eminent writer, not even Sir Walter Scott, whom I despise so entirely as I despise Shakespeare. It would be positively a relief to me to dig him up and throw stones at him."[84]

In 1905, the *New York Times* ran an article detailing a speech Shaw made about the works of Shakespeare. During the speech, Shaw outlined some of his points of contention with the bard.

First, he criticized the people who considered Shakespeare on par with God, saying a comparison of that nature was simply deplorable.

Second, Shaw echoed an argument Dryden had made that Shakespeare "was just writing what the public wanted, and that in his heart he was a pessimist."

Shaw then referred to the playwright as a "narrow-minded middle-class man." He did say he thought Shakespeare was a master when it came to prose. However, Shaw detested the more famous lines such as the "to be or not to be" passage from *Hamlet*.[85]

## King's Legacy

Stephen King's books have not been subjected to the same volume of rhetoric as Shakespeare's work. King's works are not usually studied in schools. They are not often the focus of literary criticism and theory.

However, King has been criticized for the level of gore he includes in his work, as well as the improbability of some of his plots. He also gets negative attention when he changes genres. Readers want him to only write horror, and he does not always deliver. He has written science fiction and suspense as well.

Nearly in his seventies now, King continues to publish popular books. His latest novel *Revival* is Gothic fiction.

Author and critic S.T. Joshi has stated that King's work is "a plain, bland, easy-to-read style with just the right number of scatological and sexual profanities to titillate his middle-class audience, and subscribing to the conventional morality of common people."[86]

Thus, like Shakespeare, King has been criticized for giving the people exactly what they want in the language they understand.

Joshi has also criticized the simplicity of King's plots; he claims the stories are nothing more than fantastical tales of hero versus villain.

King and Shakespeare had families. Both men had to earn a living. One path to success was by catering to the populations who might appreciate their work. If that meant using simple vocabulary and simple plots to keep the readers happy, then they were willing to write that way.

Marcus Geduld, a Shakespearean director, has also contributed to the arguments surrounding King's place in the literary canon. In 2012, Geduld published an article in *Forbes* titled "Should Stephen King Get More Credit as a Writer from Literary Critics?"

He pointed out that King was unable to craft "startling, evocative metaphors or...jarring (in a good way) sonorous effects." He later confessed his opinion that the best writers "are poets, even if they write novels and not poetry."

In his article, Geduld contrasted King's prose with that of John Updike and Cormac McCarthy. He said the other two men knew how to write arresting prose; the work of King simply got the job done.

This is the same sentiment in the criticisms of Shakespeare, who was attacked for his colloquialisms and the simplicity of some of his plots.[87]

Another criticism of Stephen King was his commercial success. As of 2014, his estimated net worth was $400 million.[88] He is viewed by the literary establishment as a celebrity novelist.

Shakespeare also died a rich man.

There is something to be said for giving the audience what they want. Both writers made this choice, and both have been well rewarded by their many satisfied fans.

# CHAPTER 8.
# MAJOR SUCCESSES, RELEVANCE, AND IMPORTANCE

While the works of Shakespeare have become a staple in the classroom, especially in the United States, some of King's books have been banned. Schools teach *Midsummer Night's Dream* and *Romeo & Juliet* rather than *Carrie* or *The Shining*. Yet, both authors remain relevant.

Shakespeare, the king of the sonnet and the most revered writer in English literature, is frequently described as a bore by high school students forced to read his work. Yet there are many reasons why it is important to continue reading Shakespeare.

His writing style teaches students how to craft a good story. He based his stories on events from his life, illustrating for readers how a good plot has more than a hint of reality. His characters were based on the people with whom he was acquainted and, therefore, he was able to bring them to life. This is important for readers to know as they work to understand stories as well as real life.

Shakespeare wrote for the people; he employed collo-quial phrases in his works to make them more accessible to his audiences. His commentary still makes sense to modern readers.

Take a look at the many phrases still in use that came from Shakespeare's work. "All that glitters is not gold" is from *The Merchant of Venice*; "Be-all and the end-all" and "come what may" are from *Macbeth*; and "Forever and a day" is from *As You Like It*.[89]

If Shakespeare's legacy teaches us anything, it is that his work is still alive and well. His works are read and studied. His plays are performed all over the world. There have been countless movies based on his plays. And there have been many movies that clothe his plots in more modern storylines.

The 1961 film *West Side Story* is one of the most notable adaptations of *Romeo & Juliet*. Although it focuses on the romance that blossoms between a Puerto Rican girl and an American boy, the plot is the same. Instead of being set in Verona, *West Side Story* takes place in New York City and portrays the conflict between two gangs, the Sharks and the Jets.

The 1994 Disney film *The Lion King* is an adaptation of *Hamlet*. Instead of taking place in the Kingdom of Denmark, the movie unfolds in an animal kingdom in

Africa. Plot similarities include the death of Mufasa, his son Simba's quest to avenge his death, and the sporadic appearance of the ghost of Mufasa to lead his son in the right direction.

The film *10 Things I Hate About You* is based on *The Taming of the Shrew*. Popular student Bianca wants to go to the prom, but her father says only if her reclusive older sister Kat finds someone to take her as well. Kat is the shrew.

In the 2006 film *She's the Man*, Viola is a budding soccer player. When she finds out the girls' soccer team is being disbanded, she poses as her brother to play on the boys' team. She is also involved in an amorous tangle as she vies for the attention of Duke, even though she had been previously linked to Justin. This is the underlying plot of *Twelfth Night*, although the era and circumstances differ.

*Hamlet* has had the most movie remakes, reappearing as new films more than fifty times since the early 1900s.

Some of the more popular adaptations include the 1948 production starring Laurence Olivier; the 1969 version in which Nicol Williamson plays Hamlet (and Anthony Hopkins plays Claudius); the 1990 version with Mel Gibson as Hamlet; and Kenneth Branagh's version in 1996. Branagh's is the only adaptation to feature the entire text; the rest were shortened versions of the script of the original play.[90]

# CHAPTER 9.
# TEN SURPRISING FACTS ABOUT WILLIAM SHAKESPEARE

## 1. HE CREATED UNIQUE WORDS AND PHRASES.

Shakespeare's affinity for language is indisputable. Many words and phrases can be credited to him. It has been estimated that he created some 1,700 words.

Among those currently in use are: "gloomy" (*Titus Andronicus*), "radiance" (*King Lear*), "hurry" (*Henry VI Part I*), and "frugal" (*Much Ado About Nothing*).[91]

He is also credited with the following common phrases:

All of a sudden Star-crossed lovers
As good luck would have it
Wild goose chase
Good riddance
Love is blind [92]

## 2. THERE'S QUITE THE INSCRIPTION ON HIS GRAVE.

When Shakespeare was buried, it was commonplace for churches to dig up graves that were already inhabited to make space for more bodies. In order to protect his own grave, Shakespeare designed an epitaph that would place a curse on anyone who dared to disturb his remains. His wishes were honored and his bones were not touched, thanks to the following message:

Good friend for Jesus' sake forbear,
To dig the dust enclosed here:

Blest be the man that spares these stones,
And curst be he that moves my bones.

### 3. HIS BELOVED GLOBE THEATER STILL EXISTS.

Shakespeare's Globe Theater was popular in London during his time. Since advertising was difficult back then, the Theater had an interesting way of notifying patrons what types of shows were playing: they utilized colored flags. If they flew a white flag, it meant a comedy was being staged. A black flag indicated a tragedy, a red flag for an historical play. When the theater burned down in 1613, it was because a canon had caught fire. No one was hurt, and the theater was rebuilt the next year.[93]

## 4. NUMBER THIRTEEN IS ASSOCIATED WITH HIS WORKS.

Considered an unlucky number, thirteen was a favorite of Shakespeare. There are thirteen suicides in his plays, including those in *Romeo & Juliet*, *Julius Caesar*, and *Hamlet*.

## 5. HE HAD A RELATIONSHIP TO THE PLANET URANUS.

Uranus has twenty-seven moons, most of them named after characters in Shakespeare's plays. The following are some of the names given to these celestial objects:[94]

Cordelia (*King Lear*)
Ophelia (*Hamlet*)
Bianca (*Taming of the Shrew*)
Cressida (*Troilus and Cressida*)
Desdemona (*Othello*)
Juliet (*Romeo & Juliet*)
Portia (*The Merchant of Venice*)
Rosalind (*As You Like It*)
Puck (*A Midsummer Night's Dream*)
Miranda (*The Tempest*)
Ariel (*The Tempest*)
Oberon (*A Midsummer Night's Dream*)
Caliban (*The Tempest*)

## 6. HE FREQUENTLY USED CURSE WORDS.

Throughout his plays, Shakespeare employed a variety of swear words, puns, and allusions to inappropriate topics. He used the word "marry" as a curse against the Virgin Mary. At the time, given the importance of religion, the word would have been equivalent to curses used today. He often alluded to syphilis;the word "err" refers to the disease. He describes the stages in this famous passage from *Timon of Athens*:

> Consumptions sow
> In hollow bones of man, strike their sharp shins,
> And mar men's spurring. Crack the lawyer's voice,
> That he may never more false title plead
> Nor sound his quillets shrilly. Hoar the flamen
> That scolds against the quality of flesh
> And not believes himself. Down with the nose,
> Down with it flat ; take the bridge quite away
> Of him that his particular to foresee
> Smells from the general weal.
> Make curled pate ruffians bald,
> And let the unscarred braggarts of the war
> Derive some pain from you. Plague all,
> That your activity may defeat and quell
> The source of all erection.[95]

### 7. ONE PLAY WAS LOST, AND ONLY RECENTLY DISCOVERED.

For decades, historians had claimed there was a missing play. The missing script had been titled *The History of*

*Cardenio* or *Cardenio*. The play had been performed in 1613, but no one had possession of a physical copy of the script. Then experts confirmed a copy of the manuscript, discovered in 2014 among the papers of Sir Humphrey McElroy, an avid collector of antiques. The estate has no intention of selling the manuscript.[96]

## 8. HE HAS A CONNECTION TO ABRAHAM LINCOLN AND JOHN WILKES BOOTH.

President Abraham Lincoln was shot on April 14, 1865, at Ford's Theater while watching the play *Our American Cousin*. He was killed by John Wilkes Booth. President Lincoln loved Shakespeare and often quoted passages from his plays. Meanwhile, his assassin was a Shakespearean actor who loved *Julius Caesar*. He had debuted at age seventeen in a production of *Richard III*. He gained much attention for his skill on stage. He had once declared, "I am determined to be a villain," the same assertion Richard makes in the play.[97]

### 9. HE HAD A CONNECTION TO ADOLF HITLER.

One of Shakespeare's fans was Adolf Hitler. Like John Wilkes Booth, Hitler was obsessed with the play *Julius Caesar*. He adapted quotes from the work and made them his own. One of his sketchbooks included a drawing he had made to recreate the stage of *Julius Caesar* and hinted at an adaptation of the play that would include members of the Third Reich. He designed a plot based on the activities of the Nazis in Germany and Italy. Hitler's version of *Julius Caesar* would have glorified his own actions in an adaptation of the Shakespearean tragedy.[98]

### 10. HE HAD AN IN WITH THE KING.

One of Shakespeare's most prominent patrons was King James I, a poet and a staunch supporter of the arts. He later became a patron of Shakespeare's theater troupe. This is why the actors were known as "The King's Men." Many scholars of literary history assert that the plot of *Macbeth* is linked to events in the King's life. There is some speculation that Shakespeare had a hand in helping to translate the King James version of the Bible, specifically Psalm 46.[99]

# CHAPTER 10.
# TEN SURPRISING FACTS ABOUT STEPHEN KING

## 1. HE HATES THE NUMBER THIRTEEN.

Stephen King suffers from triskaidekaphobia, which is fear of the number thirteen. King's phobia extends not only to the number but to multiples of thirteen as well. In order to avoid contact with the number, he has adopted various quirky behaviors and habits.

For instance, if he is ascending or descending a staircase that has thirteen steps, he will take them two at a time. If he is reading a book, he will not put the book down until he has arrived at a page that is not a multiple of thirteen. When writing, he does not end his work on a multiple of thirteen.[100]

## 2. HE CAN'T RECALL SOME OF HIS OWN BOOKS.

On May 5, 1999, the satirical publication *The Onion* featured a commentary by Stephen King entitled "I Don't Even Remember Writing *The Tommyknockers*." He tells of the time a fan once confessed her love for the novel. He could not remember the book; even the title sounded foreign to him. King wrote:

> "Anyway, when I got home, I looked up *The Tommyknockers* in this literature reference book I have and, sure enough, I wrote it in 1987... After reading the plot synopsis, I sort of remembered it, but, then again, maybe it just sounded like something else I wrote. After your 50 or 60th one, it's all kind of a blur. But if I had to venture a guess, I'd say I probably did write *The Tommyknockers*. It sounds like my kind of thing, what with this invisible evil being unleashed on a town full of innocent people and all."[101]

Due to drug and alcohol use in the 1980s, King is unable to remember writing much of the material he created during that time period. *Cujo* is another book he says he cannot recall writing.

### 3. KING HAS HAD MINOR ROLES IN THE FILM AND TELEVISION ADAPTATIONS OF HIS BOOKS.

In the 1989 production of *Pet Sematary*, King played the minister. In the 1997 television mini-series of *The Shining*, he was cast as the band leader. In the 2002 television mini-series of *Rose Red*, he played a pizza delivery man.[102]

## 4. HE DISLIKES STANLEY KUBRICK'S ADAPTATION OF *THE SHINING*.

Released in 1980, famed director Kubrick's *The Shining* has been revered, largely due to Jack Nicholson's amazing performance as the crazed Jack Torrance. King, however, had a different opinion about the movie. He was not pleased with the portrayals.

According to King, Kubrick's version included "one of the most misogynistic characters ever put on film." Kubrick's Wendy was nothing more than a damsel in distress, there to "scream and be stupid and that's not the woman that I wrote about."

King described the movie as "cold," stating that he is "not a cold guy." He stated:

> "I think one of the things people relate to in my books is this warmth, there's a reaching out and saying to the reader, 'I want you to be a part of this.' With Kubrick's 'The Shining' I felt that it was very cold, very 'We're looking at these people, but they're like ants in an anthill, aren't they doing interesting things, these little insects.'"[103]

## 5. HE WAS IN A BAND WITH OTHER FAMOUS AUTHORS.

From 1994 to 2012, a rock band called the Rock Bottom Remainders performed in various venues to raise money for charities. The band had many lineups throughout those years including Mitch Albom, Amy Tan, Ridley Pearson, and James McBride.

King was an original member of the band and played rhythm guitar. The authors that made up the band have sold a total of 350 million books and released forty *New York Times* #1 Bestsellers. They were also successful in raising around $2 million to benefit charities.[104]

## 6. RICHARD BACHMAN AND JOHN SWITHEN ARE KING'S TWO PEN NAMES.

When the marketplace had a handful of his novels to choose from, King and his publisher agreed he would also write books under a pen name. They did not want the success of his sales to be determined solely by his identity.

Richard Bachman published the novels *Rage* in 1977, *The Long Walk* in 1979, *Roadwork* in 1981, and *The Running Man* in 1982. This allowed King to publish more than one book a year without overwhelming audiences.[105]

King used the pseudonym John Swithen when he published the short story "The Fifth Quarter" in 1972.

## 7. HE AVOIDS ADVERBS.

In his terrific book *On Writing: A Memoir on the Craft*, the author advises writers to avoid the excessive use of adverbs. King's own sentences are clear-cut and to the point, and he does not weaken meanings or dilute his ideas with weak words. He says use of adverbs is bad writing and explains that bad writing stems from fear:

> I'm convinced that fear is at the root of most bad writing. If one is writing for one's own pleasure, that fear may be mild — timidity is the word I've used here. If, however, one is working under deadline — a school paper, a newspaper article, the SAT writing sample — that fear may be intense. Dumbo got airborne with the help of a magic feather; you may feel the urge to grasp a passive verb or one of those nasty adverbs for the same reason. Just remember before you do that Dumbo didn't need the feather; the magic was in him.[106]

## 8. HE HAS A CONTROVERSIAL POSITION ON TAXATION.

Although the author's net worth is estimated to be somewhere around $400 million, King believes that all wealthy Americans should pay higher taxes.

He is not quiet about his opinion, either. In 2012, he wrote a scathing op-ed piece for *The Daily Beast* in which he belittled the rich folks who want to pay lower taxes.

King also made public his opinion about the "right wing of the Republican Party" that has taken to defending wealthy Americans against increased taxes. In his piece, he posed the question:

> If I hit the movie jackpot —as I have, from time to time —and own a piece of a film that grosses $200 million, what am I going to do with it? Buy another radio station? I don't think so, since I'm losing my shirt on the ones I own already.[107]

### 9. AN IMPROMPTU BOOK SIGNING GOT HIM IN TROUBLE.

After stepping into an Australian bookstore in 2007, King decided that he would sign fans' copies of his books. The owner of the Alice Springs' bookstore thought he was vandalizing her stock and wanted to have him arrested.[108]

### 10. THE STANLEY HOTEL CONTINUES THE LEGACY.

The Stanley Hotel in Estes Park, Colorado, one of the inspirations for *The Shining*, runs on continuous loop on every television set in all of their 140 guest rooms the uncut version of the film. The movie plays all day and all night. The hotel was the setting for the Overlook Hotel when King directed the television mini-series in 1997.[109]

# WHAT'S NEXT?

Did you enjoy this mashup? Are you suddenly making new connections in your own mind, cool mashups between other famous people in history? Want to share your ideas with us?

This book is one in a series of teen-friendly mashup books that compare famous figures and provide interesting information about their lives. If you have a suggestion for a new mashup book, please contact us here:

melissa@networlding.com
http://facebook.com/mashupsbooks

If you liked this book, read the other books in the Masters Mashups series to learn about:

Marie Antoinette, former Queen of France,
and Madonna, the Queen of Pop:
http://www.amazon.com/dp/B00QFXTA1

Princess Grace, Pricess Diana, and Princess Kate:

http://amzn.com/B00QXHW2AU

Sleeping Beauty and Beyoncé:
http://amzn.com/B00QXHW2AU

If you enjoyed the book, please take the time to write a review on Amazon or Goodreads. Even a short one will be greatly appreciated. Tell your classmates, tell your parents, tell your friends about Masters Mashups. These books are the fun way to learn history!

Note that all proceeds from our mashup books go to apprenticing young adults interested in writing and publishing. We provide internships for students in digital publishing here at Networlding Publishing. The Masters Mashups series helps make this opportunity possible for young writers, editors, and readers.

# ENDNOTES

1    http://www.madmusic.com/song_details.aspx?SongID=897

2    http://www.stratford.edu/tech_talk/shows/2014/06-28-2014

3    http://education-portal.com/academy/lesson/john-polidoris-the-vampyre-summary-analysis-quiz.html#lesson

4    http://www.latimes.com/books/la-et-book4-2010mar04-story.html

5    http://www.imdb.com/title/tt1611224/

6    https://www.goodreads.com/shelf/show/mashup

7    http://seattletimes.com/html/books/2023452962_mooreserpentvenicexml.html

8    Doescher, Ian. William Shakespeare's Star Wars: verily, a new hope. Philadelphia, PA: Quirk Books, 2013. Print. <http://www.bibme.org/>

9    http://goodcomics.comicbookresources.com/2012/09/20/the-line-it-is-drawn-107-comic-book-characters-mashed-up-with-stephen-king-stories/

10   http://stephenking.com/the_author.html

11   http://www.history.com/news/history-lists/10-things-you-didnt-know-about-william-shakespeare

12   http://www.history.com/news/history-lists/10-things-you-didnt-know-about-william-shakespeare

13   http://stephenking.com/the_author.html

14   http://www.lastwritesdmd.com/the-glass-floor-reviewed-by-craig-garrett/

15 http://www.shakespeare-online.com/plays/violenceinshakespeare.html

16 http://flash.sonypictures.com/downloads/movies/carrie/Carrie-StephenKing_AnchorMM_Excerpt.pdf

17 http://www.dailymail.co.uk/tvshowbiz/article-1178151/Stephen-Kings-Real-Horror-Story-How-novelists-addiction-drink-drugs-nearly-killed-him.html

18 http://www.opensourceshakespeare.org/views/plays/play_view.php?WorkID=richard3&Act=5&Scene=3&Scope=scene

19 http://www.bbc.co.uk/bitesize/higher/english/macbeth/background/revision/1/

20 http://www.poetryfoundation.org/poem/247636

21 http://www.businessinsider.com/school-shootings-drove-stephen-king-to-take-rage-off-shelves-2014-3

22 http://www.dailymail.co.uk/tvshowbiz/article-1178151/Stephen-Kings-Real-Horror-Story-How-novelists-addiction-drink-drugs-nearly-killed-him.html

23 http://books.google.com/books?id=HjURCQHV4wAC&pg=PR10&lpg=PR10&dq=Shakespeare+and+Stephen+King&source=bl&ots=qmloTiLX14&sig=MGJNddKnHLiD4DibAsTPUNZbBF4&hl=en&sa=X&ei=iEH6U5GdAsuOyASE7IKYDQ&ved=0CB0Q6AEwADgK#v=onepage&q=Shakespeare%20and%20Stephen%20King&f=false

24 http://blogs.amctv.com/movie-blog/2008/06/stand-by-me-stephen-king/

25 https://archive.org/details/OTRR_Dimension_X_Singles

26 http://books.google.com/books?id=HjURCQHV4wAC&pg=PR10&lpg=PR10&dq=Shakespeare+and+Stephen+King&source=bl&ots=qmloTiLX14&sig=MGJNddKnHLiD4DibAsTPUNZbBF4&hl=en&sa=X&ei=iEH6U5GdAsuOyASE7IKYDQ&ved=0CB0Q6AEwADgK#v=onepage&q=Shakespeare%20and%20Stephen%20King&f=false

27 http://www.nytimes.com/2013/06/26/books/richard-matheson-writer-of-haunted-science-fiction-and-horror-dies-at-87.html?_r=0

28 http://grantland.com/hollywood-prospectus/r-i-p-sci-fi-giant-richard-matheson-author-of-i-am-legend/

29   http://www.theblackelf.com/2012/08/daves-rag-by-stephen-king/

30   http://www.theshakespeareconspiracy.com/shakespearevsmarlowe.html

31   http://www.shakespeare-navigators.com/dream/T.1.1.html

32   http://shakespeare.mit.edu/richardiii/richardiii.5.3.html

33   http://www.bartleby.com/19/2/24.html

34   http://themarlowestudies.org/literarysimilarities.html

35   http://www.shakespeare-online.com/faq/shakespeareinspired.html

36   http://faculty.history.wisc.edu/sommerville/123/123%20263%201580s%20&%2090s.htm

37   http://www.monologuearchive.com/s/shakespeare_020.html

38   https://www.biblegateway.com/passage/?search=Ephesians+5%3A22-33&version=KJV

39   https://www.biblegateway.com/passage/?search=2+Corinthians+11%3A13-14&version=NKJV

40   http://nfs.sparknotes.com/macbeth/page_20.html

41   http://www.opensourceshakespeare.org/views/plays/play_view.php?WorkID=tempest&Act=1&Scene=2&Scope=scene

42   http://www.ox.ac.uk/media/news_stories/2013/131102.html

43   http://www.canadianshakespeares.ca/folio/Sources/romeusandjuliet.pdf

44   http://shakespeare.mit.edu/romeo_juliet/romeo_juliet.1.0.html

45   http://www.nybooks.com/articles/archives/2004/oct/21/the-death-of-hamnet-and-the-making-of-hamlet/

46   http://www.shakespeare-online.com/sonnets/shakespearepetrarch.html

47   http://stephenking.com/faq.html

48   http://stephenking.com/library/novel/carrie_inspiration.html

49   http://stephenking.wikia.com/wiki/Rage

50  http://books.google.com/books?id=8VnJLu3AvvQC&printsec=
    frontcover&dq=The+Shining&hl=en&sa=X&ei=Oy36U4mpFNL
    9yQSg3YHwAQ&ved=0CB8Q6AEwAA#v=onepage&q=The%20
    Shining&f=false

51  http://stephenking.com/library/novel/it_inspiration.html

52  http://stephenking.com/library/novel/christine_inspiration.html

53  http://www.shakespeare-online.com/biography/
    shakespeareactor.html

54  http://www.shakespeare-online.com/biography/
    shakespeareactor.html

55  http://www.shakespeare-online.com/biography/
    shakespeareactor.html

56  http://www.shakespeare-online.com/biography/
    shakespeareactor.html

57  http://absoluteshakespeare.com/trivia/globe/globe.htm

58  http://awood.blogspot.com/2012/05/stephen-king-long-walk-as-
    richard.html

59  http://home.comcast.net/~antaylor1/alabestteens.html

60  http://books.google.com/books?id=HjURCQHV4wAC&pg=PR10&l
    pg=PR10&dq=Shakespeare+and+Stephen+King&source=bl&ots
    =qmloTiLX14&sig=MGJNddKnHLiD4DibAsTPUNZbBF4&hl=en&sa
    =X&ei=iEH6U5GdAsuOyASE7IKYDQ&ved=0CB0Q6AEwADgK#v=o
    nepage&q=Shakespeare%20and%20Stephen%20King&f=false

61  http://books.google.com/books?id=HjURCQHV4wAC&pg=PR10&l
    pg=PR10&dq=Shakespeare+and+Stephen+King&source=bl&ots
    =qmloTiLX14&sig=MGJNddKnHLiD4DibAsTPUNZbBF4&hl=en&sa
    =X&ei=iEH6U5GdAsuOyASE7IKYDQ&ved=0CB0Q6AEwADgK#v=o
    nepage&q=Shakespeare%20and%20Stephen%20King&f=false

62  http://mentalfloss.com/article/53235/how-stephen-kings-wife-
    saved-carrie-and-launched-his-career

63  https://www.goodreads.com/work/quotes/150292-on-writing-a-
    memoir-of-the-craft

64  http://www.hollywoodreporter.com/heat-vision/stephen-kings-be-
    adapted-by-334899

65    Mabillard, Amanda. Shakespeare of Stratford: Shakespeare's Marriage. Shakespeare Online. 20 Aug. 2000. <http://www.shakespeare-online.com/biography/shakespearemarriage.html>.

66    http://www.shakespeare-online.com/biography/deathofshakespeare.html

67    http://www.shakespeare-online.com/sonnets/20.html

68    http://www.shakespeare-online.com/sonnets/126.html

69    http://www.spectatornews.com/currents/2012/02/16/queens-of-the-ball/

70    http://www.fordham.edu/halsall/pwh/englaw.asp

71    http://books.google.com/books?id=d999Z2KbZJYC&printsec=frontcover&dq=on+writing+by+stephen+king&hl=en&sa=X&ei=Ae8EVK3rDsPJgwTV3lDgBw&ved=0CDMQ6wEwAA#v=onepage&q=on%20writing%20by%20stephen%20king&f=false

72    http://www.people.com/people/archive/article/0,,20079300,00.html

73    http://www.nytimes.com/2013/08/04/magazine/stephen-kings-family-business.html?pagewanted=all&_r=0

74    http://www.addictioninfo.org/articles/4245/1/Stephen-King-overcame-alcohol-and-drug-addiction/Page1.html

75    http://www.theguardian.com/books/2000/sep/24/stephenking.fiction

76    http://www.theguardian.com/books/2000/oct/01/stephenking.fiction1

77    http://stephenking.com/library/novel/lisey_s_story.html

78    http://bangordailynews.com/2013/03/19/news/bangor/stephen-and-tabitha-king-offer-to-cover-one-third-of-9-million-bangor-library-renovation-if-library-finds-ways-to-foot-the-rest-of-the-bill/

79    http://shakespeare.about.com/od/shakespeareslife/a/shakespeare-death.htm

80    http://www.bartleby.com/39/23.html

81    http://andromeda.rutgers.edu/~jlynch/Texts/drampoet.html

82 http://www.britannica.com/shakespeare/article-232333

83 http://www.infoplease.com/encyclopedia/people/shakespeare-william-critical-opinion.html

84 http://mentalfloss.com/article/22551/quick-10-10-people-who-hate-shakespeare

85 http://query.nytimes.com/mem/archive-free/pdf?res=9904E4DB1E3DE633A2575BC2A9629C946497D6CF

86 http://open.salon.com/blog/thehorror/2013/09/02/critical_mass_why_stephen_king_annoys_critics_part_2

87 http://www.forbes.com/sites/quora/2012/02/08/should-stephen-king-get-more-credit-as-a-writer-from-literary-critics/

88 http://www.therichest.com/celebnetworth/celeb/authors/stephen-king-net-worth/

89 http://www.pathguy.com/shakeswo.htm

90 http://petergalenmassey.com/2012/06/29/9-best-hamlet-movies-shakespeare/

91 http://www.huffingtonpost.com/2014/01/14/shakespeare-words_n_4590819.html

92 http://www.phrases.org.uk/meanings/phrases-sayings-shakespeare.html

93 http://www.nosweatshakespeare.com/resources/shakespeare-globe-facts/

94 http://www.bobthealien.co.uk/uranusmoons.htm

95 http://shakespeare.revues.org/1141

96 http://worldnewsdailyreport.com/london-lost-play-of-shakespeare-discovered-in-family-heirloom/

97 http://www.biography.com/people/john-wilkes-booth-9219681#acting-career

98 http://www.telegraph.co.uk/culture/theatre/william-shakespeare/10755197/Shakespeare-10-things-you-didnt-know.html

99 http://communities.washingtontimes.com/neighborhood/worlds-best-selling-book/2011/jul/16/william-shakespeare-his-role-king-james-bible-tran/

100 http://www.nytimes.com/books/97/03/09/lifetimes/kin-v-friday13th.html

101 http://www.theonion.com/articles/i-dont-even-remember-writing-the-tommyknockers,10929/

102 http://stephenking.com/library/appearance/index_old-new.html

103 http://blogs.indiewire.com/theplaylist/stephen-king-says-wendy-in-kubricks-the-shining-is-one-of-the-most-misogynistic-characters-ever-put-on-film-20130919

104 http://www.rockbottomremainders.com/

105 http://stephenking.com/library/bachman_novel/

106 http://www.brainpickings.org/index.php/2013/03/13/stephen-king-on-adverbs/

107 http://www.rawstory.com/rs/2012/04/30/stephen-king-tells-rich-people-upset-over-tax-increases-tough-st/

108 http://news.bbc.co.uk/2/hi/entertainment/6949300.stm

109 http://www.venere.com/blog/the-stanley-hotel-576729/

www.ingramcontent.com/pod-product-compliance
Lightning Source LLC
Chambersburg PA
CBHW050352280326
41933CB00010BA/1433